FORECASTING

Dr Jennifer L. Castle is a Tutorial Fellow in Economics at Magdalen College, Oxford University, and a Research Fellow at the Institute for New Economic Thinking at the Oxford Martin School. She previously held a British Academy Postdoctoral Research Fellowship at Nuffield College, Oxford. She is a former director of the International Institute of Forecasters, and has contributed to the field of forecasting from both theoretical and practical approaches, publishing in leading journals and contributing to the development of several software packages.

Michael P. Clements is Professor of Econometrics at the ICMA Centre, Henley Business School, University of Reading, and is an Associate Member of the Institute for New Economic Thinking at the Oxford Martin School, University of Oxford. He obtained a DPhil in Econometrics from Nuffield College, University of Oxford, before moving to Warwick University Economics Department as a Research Fellow, and moved to Reading in 2013. He is a Distinguished Author of the *Journal of Applied Econometrics*, an Honorary Fellow of the International Institute of Forecasters, and Series Editor of the Palgrave Texts in Econometrics and Palgrave Advanced Texts in Econometrics. He has over 70 articles in refereed academic journals, 4 books, 2 edited books, and 12 book chapters.

Sir David F. Hendry, Kt, is a Senior Research Fellow of Nuffield College, Oxford University, and co-director of the Program in Economic Modeling at the Institute for New Economic Thinking and of Climate Econometrics, both at the Oxford Martin School. He was previously Professor of Economics at Oxford University and Professor of Econometrics, London School of Economics. He was knighted in 2009, and received a Lifetime Achievement Award from the Economic and Social Research Council in 2014. He is a Fellow of the British Academy, the Royal Society of Edinburgh, the Econometric Society, the Academy of Social Sciences, *Econometric Reviews*, and the *Journal of Econometrics*. Sir David is also an Honorary Vice-President and a past President of the Royal Economic Society, a Foreign Honorary Member of the American Economic Association and the American Academy of Arts and Sciences, as well as an Honorary Fellow of the International Institute of Forecasters. He has been awarded 8 Honorary Doctorates, is listed by the ISI as one of the world's 200 most cited economists, is a Thomson Reuters Citation Laureate, and has received the

T0326841

Guy Medal in Bronze from the Royal Statistical Society. He has published more than 200 papers and 25 books on econometric methods, theory, modeling, and history; numerical techniques; econometric computing; empirical economics; and economic forecasting, for which he was awarded the Isaac Kerstenetzky Scholarly Achievement Award in 2012. His latest book, *Introductory Macro-econometrics: A New Approach*, Timberlake Consultants, 2015, focuses on the concepts, tools and techniques needed to model aggregate economic data, implementing automated general-to-specific model selection.

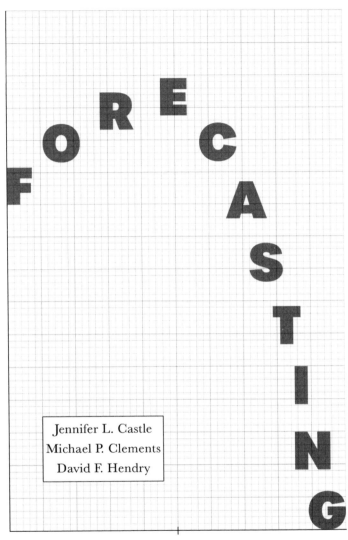

FORECASTING

Jennifer L. Castle
Michael P. Clements
David F. Hendry

An Essential Introduction

YALE UNVERSITY PRESS
NEW HAVEN AND LONDON

Copyright © 2019 Jennifer L. Castle, Michael P. Clements and David F. Hendry

All rights reserved. This book may not be reproduced in whole or in part, in any form (beyond that copying permitted by Sections 107 and 108 of the U.S. Copyright Law and except by reviewers for the public press) without written permission from the publishers.

For information about this and other Yale University Press publications,
please contact:
U.S. Office: sales.press@yale.edu yalebooks.com
Europe Office: sales@yaleup.co.uk yalebooks.co.uk

This book has been composed in LaTeX using MikTex
Set in Times by David F. Hendry

Printed in Great Britain by CPI Group (UK) Ltd, Croydon, CR0 4YY

Library of Congress Control Number: 2019934600

ISBN 978-0-300-24466-3

A catalogue record for this book is available from the British Library.

10 9 8 7 6 5 4 3 2 1

Contents

Figures

Preface

> Trying to predict the future is a mug's game. But ... we need
> to have some sort of idea of what the future's actually going
> to be like because we are going to have to live there, probably
> next week.
>
> Douglas Adams, *The Salmon of Doubt*, Basingstoke: Macmillan, 2002.

The authors have spent about 80 person years between them researching the theory underlying forecasting, especially as it occurs in economics. When the third author was a Special Adviser to the House of Commons Select Committee on the Treasury and Civil Service Enquiry into Official Economic Forecasting in 1991, he noted the proliferation of forecasts and of post-mortems of their performance, but the almost complete absence of a general theory of forecasting relevant to the ever changing real world. Since then, we have sought to establish such a theory, and believe we have succeeded, yielding many insights into when forecasts were likely to go awry, as well as how to mitigate the most persistent mistakes.

All but a few of the resulting publications are at a technical and mathematical level that make their findings inaccessible to non-specialists. This is unfortunate, as a better understanding of the uncertainty surrounding forecasts, applicable to many disciplines, would be valuable in everyday life. One introduction is *Understanding Economic Forecasts* by Hendry and Neil Ericsson, MIT Press 2001. A more recent less technical explanation, despite its title, is *All Change! The Implications of Non-stationarity for Empirical Modelling, Forecasting and Policy*, by Hendry and Felix Pretis, Oxford Martin School Policy Paper, 2016: see http://www.oxfordmartin.ox.ac.uk/publications/view/2318.

This book is a new attempt to explain forecasting, drawing on the analogy of a poor motorist facing many trials and tribulations on her journey, first sketched in 'Forecasting Pitfalls', *Bulletin of EU and US Inflation and Macroeconomic Analysis*, 100th Issue, 2003, currently available online at https://e-revistas.uc3m.es/index.php/BIMA/article/view/2634. Most of her difficulties in accurately forecasting her arrival time have counterparts facing forecasters everywhere. We hope this 'homely' setting of an everyday activity will clarify the general issues and concepts of this important topic. Any mathematics relating textual explanations to equations of the form used in forecasting occur in boxed material, so can be skipped by those not wishing to explore such links.

Acknowledgments

Financial support from the Robertson Foundation and the Institute for New Economic Thinking is gratefully acknowledged.

We are indebted to Neil R. Ericsson, Vivien L. Hendry, Andrew B. Martinez, John N.J. Muellbauer, Bent Nielsen, Dilek Önkal, Felix Pretis, J. James Reade and Angela Wenham as well as two anonymous referees for helpful comments on earlier drafts.

We thank Paul Lowe and Lena Boneva at the Bank of England for granting us permission to use material and the data from the paper 'Evaluating UK point and density forecasts from an estimated DSGE model: the role of off-model information over the financial crisis', by Nicholas Fawcett, Lena Körber, Riccardo M. Masolo and Matt Waldron, Bank of England Staff Working Paper No. 538.

We are grateful to Taiba Batool of Yale University Press for suggesting this project to communicate at least some of the findings about economic forecasting that have been discovered over the last 25 years or so, and her encouragement to complete it.

We are also grateful to Nicholas Fawcett, Andrew B. Martinez and Felix Pretis for their kind permission to use material from their various research publications.

The book was originally typeset with help from Jurgen Doornik and Bent Nielsen using MikTex, MacTeX and OxEdit. Except when otherwise stated, illustrations and numerical computations used *OxMetrics* (see Jurgen A. Doornik, *OxMetrics: An Interface to Empirical Modelling*, Timberlake Consultants Press, London, 2018) and *PcGive* (see J.A. Doornik and D.F. Hendry, *Empirical Econometric Modelling using PcGive*, Timberlake Consultants Press, London, 2018).

Chapter 1

Why do we need forecasts?

A forecast is any statement about the future.
Clements and Hendry, *Forecasting Economic Time Series*, Cambridge University Press, 1998.

What is a forecast?

Statements about the future can take many forms. For example, 'tomorrow it will rain heavily', which may be well based using the science of meteorology, or just a causal remark by a neighbor looking at the sky. Many other examples occur in everyday life: 'the stock market will rise 1% next week'; 'your flight will arrive on time'; and so on. Some forecasts are vague whereas others are relatively precise; some concern the near term, and some the distant future. Not all forecasts are well based, such as guessing—'the first extraterrestrial will land on Earth on 1 January 2045'. This book will focus on explaining forecasts based on 'rules' that can be checked for their competence. While making statements about the future is easy, producing competent forecasts is a much harder task.

But pause for a moment: the word 'forecast' is composed of 'fore', a shortened form of before, denoting 'in advance', and 'cast', which has more dubious connotations. Humans cast nets and fishing lines in the hope of catching fish; or cast dice in the hope of winning a gambling game; and horoscopes are cast, as are spells in fantasy fiction and fairy tales. All a bit chancy. However, bronze statues are also cast, so the word could entail a productive process. Nevertheless, chance is central to forecasting in all disciplines and reflects the obvious feature that forecasts can, and often do, differ from outcomes. As we will discuss, forecasts should be accompanied by some measure of how uncertain they are—even though that uncertainty may itself be uncertain! So we should really say 'we are fairly sure that tomorrow it will rain heavily' or 'tomorrow it is very likely to rain heavily', assuming that is indeed what the observations of an incoming storm suggest.

Weather forecasting was introduced by Robert Fitzroy in 1859, who devised a storm warning system that was the prototype of the modern weather forecast. If a storm was not forecast but happened, ships sank with loss of life; and if a storm was forecast but did not happen, ships stayed in port unnecessarily and led to economic losses. Conversely, correctly forecasting a perfect day allowed ships to sail safely, or being right about a storm occurring avoided deaths and economic losses. Consequently, there were two ways of being successful, but also two of failing, and those failures were always heavily criticized. Unfortunately, the difficulties in making 'successful' forecasts led Fitzroy to commit suicide in 1865. Previously, Fitzroy had captained the *Beagle* on which Charles Darwin made his historic 1831–36 round-the-world voyage, and during which Fitzroy argued with Darwin against Darwin's growing doubts about Creationism. Fitzroy was also governor of New Zealand, 1843–45, where he supported Māori land claims as valid. He later strongly opposed Darwin's work, adding to his mental difficulties.

Weather forecasting accuracy has improved enormously since Fitzroy's first attempts, now based on physical theories of the atmosphere, oceans, land and the sun's energy, supported by many millions of observations of current and immediate past weather. But there can still be major misses, as with the famous failure to forecast the terrible October 1987 storm in the United Kingdom when about 15,000,000 trees were blown down and many lives were lost.

Some insights into the challenges facing the economic forecaster are provided by the example of casting two six-faced dice that are perfect cubes. That games of chance can be used to help explain probability should not come as a surprise. Historically, the development of probability theory was motivated by the needs of the gambler. However, reader, do not worry if you find probability hard to fathom: the famous French mathematician Jean le Rond d'Alembert thought that when tossing a penny twice, the probability of 2 heads, 2 tails and a head & a tail were all one-third! You could lose a lot of money betting on those incorrect odds. For a throw of two dice, we can calculate all the possible outcomes, of which there are 36. Provided the dice are 'fair' (so perfectly balanced), throwing two sixes together has one chance in 36. There is a 50-50 chance that the outcome of adding the digits on the two faces is an odd number, and so on. Such calculations are certain in theory, but they tell us nothing about what the next throw will yield. Consider a run of 10 throws where the sum is an odd number for each throw. Can you conclude the dice are loaded? Although such a sequence will only happen rarely, it will occur on average about once in every 1024 occasions that a balanced pair are fairly thrown 10 times in a row. Now think how many millions of dice have been thrown over the years: such 'rare' outcomes must have happened often. However, it would take a reckless gambler to forecast that every one of the *next* 10 throws on any given day will sum to an odd number, unless of course, the dice are loaded in a way they know. Such a bet should make you suspicious. We've all seen the classic 'cowboy' movies—there are potentially dangerous outcomes for those gambling with loaded dice once they are discovered.

This tale has three motivations. The first is to emphasize how uncertain many events are in advance, even when all possible outcomes are known. Uncertainty is even greater when no-one knows the complete set of possibilities—a crucial issue for forecasters. The second concerns how to measure the uncertainty of a forecast, or a sequence of forecasts. This is possible in a setting like our dice example, but is vastly more difficult when the future may hold surprises. The third is to wonder if we can load the 'dice' in our favor when forecasting, not by cheating, but by clever approaches. All three aspects of the tale will be major themes of the book.

Why do we need forecasts?

Some of our most interesting conversations can be with taxi drivers. When Hendry (the third author) was in Oslo to present a seminar at Norges Bank (the Central Bank of Norway) on 'Economic Forecasting', his taxi driver expressed skepticism about the topic, remarking that 'your lectures on forecasting are pointless'. Hendry responded, 'so why are you out this morning: have you not forecast finding sufficient potential customers?' It transpired the taxi driver was actually quite good at forecasting when and where to seek trade, *but had never thought of it that way*. He then conceded that perhaps forecasting was possible, and indeed necessary.

Forecasts are needed in all walks of life for facilitating decisions: how long will this journey take?; should I buy in this shop or look further for a lower price?; will it rain today?; is he/she the correct marriage partner?; and so on. In economics, forecasts are essential to formulate planning and policy. Consequently, we need to explore how forecasts are made, often by forecasting models that are developed from limited available data. In many situations, a story is needed with forecasts to make them 'sellable'. Raw numbers are not sufficient. People usually 'buy into' the forecasts only if there is an accompanying narrative that they can relate to: central banks often emphasize their discussions of the likely outcomes rather than the numerical forecasts.

A brief history of forecasting

Records of attempts by humanity to forecast important events date back to the origins of writing, but forecasting almost surely predates such records. Hunter–gatherer groups must have needed to forecast where game, or predators, might be, and where to find edible plants and water sources at different times of the year. To do so, they must have formed views about likely times for rain and drought as well as the changing seasons. In antiquity, Babylonians tracked the annual evolution of the night sky, presumably to facilitate planting and harvesting of crops. Ancient Egyptians had devices for forecasting the impacts of the annual floods of the river

Nile, essential for irrigating and refreshing their fields with new soil. But there are some more questionable ancient attempts such as the Oracles of Delphi, who provided many early examples of (usually) ambiguous forecasts, followed in the 16th Century by Nostradamus, as well as Cassandra of Troy who it was claimed could see the future but was never believed (so an economist would advise her to predict the opposite. . .).

Perhaps one of the earliest attempts at statistical forecasting was by the English economist, Sir William Petty, during the 17th Century.[1] In his major contributions to quantitative economics, which he termed political arithmetic, Petty attempted to quantify macroeconomic variables. In doing so, he thought he had observed a seven-year 'business cycle'. This would provide the basis for systematic economic forecasts, although Petty does not seem to have followed through to do so. But such forecasts would have been doomed to failure as historically, business cycles 'vary greatly in duration and intensity' as Victor Zarnowitz has shown.[2]

Above we noted a brief history of weather forecasting in the latter half of the 19th Century, which has since become a major industry, with additional efforts at forecasting the intensity and landfall of hurricanes and other tropical cyclones, the trajectories of tornados, as well as the potential paths of tsunamis once they have been triggered, and the impacts of volcanic eruptions. Nevertheless, probably the greatest effort is devoted to economic, and especially financial, forecasting.

The embryonic forecasting industry in the United States at the start of the 20th Century blossomed in the 1920s, adopting the then 'latest methods' of business barometers and ABC curves proposed by Warren Persons. Despite the inclusion of luminaries such as Irving Fisher, almost all failed to forecast the Great Depression beginning in 1929, with the exception of Roger Babson. Babson then also lost credibility by repeatedly forecasting its end—which failed to materialize.[3] However, a later follow up using

---

[1] Ted McCormick, *William Petty: And the Ambitions of Political Arithmetic*, Oxford University Press, 2009.

[2] V. Zarnowitz, (2004) 'An important subject in need of much new research', *Journal of Business Cycle Measurement and Analysis* **1**.

[3] Walter Friedman, *Fortune Tellers: The Story of America's First Economic Forecasters*, Princeton University Press, 2014, provides an early history of forecasting in the USA.

modern forecasting approaches was still unable to forecast the sharp downturn in 1930, so the forecasters at the time should not be judged harshly.[4]

That debacle did lead to greatly increased economic data collection, further extended during and after World War II. It also led to the development of better statistical methods for economic modeling in an attempt to understand what had gone wrong. Nevertheless, economic forecasts have not had unmitigated success since. When they are most needed because of sudden large shocks to the economy, forecasts can be seriously awry, as happened most recently in 2008–9. We call such episodes 'forecast failure', referring to outcomes deviating from forecasts by a greater magnitude than could be reasonably expected on the basis of the past performance of the method being used.

Explaining the sources of forecast failure will be an important aspect of our book, but it is not uniquely an economic problem. Forecast failure abounds in a wide range of disciplines. Take Sir Erasmus Wilson, an Oxford Professor and dermatologist, who stated, 'when the Paris Exhibition closes, electric light will close with it and no more be heard of'.[5] Or the New York Times in 1936 printing, 'a rocket will never be able to leave the Earth's atmosphere'.[6] We have already noted the 1987 weather forecast blunder; and will later discuss the famous failed Moon landing of 1970 by Apollo 13, a drama since made into a film.

Why are forecasts uncertain?

Variability in many aspects of life is reasonably well described by what is called a Normal distribution. Its ubiquity partly explains its name, although it is also called a Gaussian distribution after the great mathematician who first described it. This is the (in)famous 'bell curve'. Human heights are approximately Normally distributed. If one measured the

---

[4]See Kathryn Dominguez, Ray Fair and Matthew Shapiro (1988) https://fairmodel.econ.yale.edu/rayfair/pdf/1988c200.pdf.

[5]See, e.g., John Wade, *The Ingenious Victorians: Weird and Wonderful Ideas from the Age of Innovation*, Pen and Sword Books, 2016.

[6]*The New York Times*, January 13, 1920. The *Times* offered a retraction on July 17, 1969, as Apollo 11 was on its way to the Moon.

height of every adult in the UK (say) there would be a preponderance of heights near the middle of the distribution, and fewer extremely tall or very short individuals. For ease of calculation, assume the most common height is 6 feet (1.83 meters), the shortest 4 feet (1.22 meters) and the tallest 8 feet (2.44 meters). The spread between shortest and tallest is 2/3rds of the middle height, so the range is not too great.

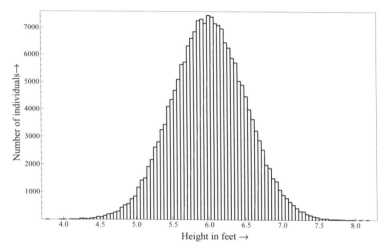

Figure 1.1: A histogram illustrating 200,000 artificial heights.

In the UK, the average height for men is 5ft 10in (1.78 meters) and for women is 5ft 5in (1.65 meters).[7] The world's tallest recorded man stood almost 9 feet (2.72 meters) high. The number of individuals measured at each height can be collected in groups, or bins, of say 1/2 inch (0.012 meter), for example one from 5ft 3.5in to 5ft 4in and so on. Then the numbers in each bin can be graphed in what is called a histogram, as in Figure 1.1, although we have used computer generated numbers, not real heights.

---

[7]Statistics taken from *A century of trends in adult human height*, 2016. https://www.ncbi.nlm.nih.gov/pubmed/27458798.

Histograms show the probabilities of the outcomes being in different intervals. The vertical axis shows that there are approximately 7000 people in each of the seven bins near the peak of the histogram, which are close to 6 feet tall. The horizontal axis shows the height at the center of each bin, reported at 6 inch (0.15 meter) intervals although each bin is 1/2 inch wide. When there are many millions of individuals in the random sample, the distribution of heights will become close to a Normal.

Figure 1.2 shows a 'standard' Normal distribution, namely one centered on zero, but imagine the 0 corresponds to the most common height of 6 feet. The horizontal axis records the number of units around the center, and the vertical axis shows how 'dense' the distribution is at each point, namely how likely we are to find an individual at that distance from the center. Although often called a distribution, as we will do, Figure 1.2 really shows a 'density' where deviations from the center are standardized in units of 1. Please study Figure 1.2 carefully: it is important to understanding forecast uncertainty.

Roughly 66% of outcomes will lie between −1 and +1, 95% of outcomes between −2 and +2, and outcomes outside the range −3 to +3 (called the tails of the distribution) are rather unlikely, as can be seen by the closeness to zero of the distribution outside that region. 'Randomly' picking an individual from a Normal distribution such as Figure 1.2 means that anyone is just as likely to be picked as anyone else. While that outcome will be uncertain, it is most likely to be near the center, rather than in the tail, as shown by 'X marks the spot' in the figure. But, like our 10 successive outcomes of an odd sum when throwing the two dice, some 'extreme' outcomes will occur: very tall and very short individuals exist.

A distribution like that in Figure 1.2 has three key features. First, its location, here centered on zero. Second, its spread, here measured in units of 1, which is why it is called 'standard'. Third, its shape, namely Normal in our figure, or 'bell shaped'.

There are several reasonable ways to measure the center of a distribution. If we ordered every adult from the smallest upward, then the middle individual could be taken as the center, called the median. Alternatively, we could find the most common height, called the mode, which corresponds to the peak of the distribution. Finally, one could calculate the

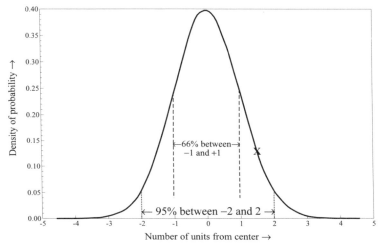

Figure 1.2: A 'standard' Normal distribution illustrating uncertainty in outcomes.

arithmetic average of all the heights, called the mean. When the distribution is Normal, all three coincide, so the mean, median and mode in Figure 1.2 are all zero (or 6 feet if centered for our assumption about heights).

There are also a number of plausible ways to measure the spread. A commonly used measure is called the *variance* as it seeks to describe the variability around the center. However, the one we will focus on is the square root of the variance, called the standard deviation, again a name chosen to reflect deviations from the center in standard units. When the units being studied are in feet, miles, or $millions, the standard deviation is correspondingly in feet, miles, or $millions. The standard deviation in Figure 1.2 is 1, which would translate to about 6 inches in the original height measures.

Often a 'random' sample is drawn from a population, and its characteristics are used to infer those of the underlying population. Provided we had a sufficiently large sample, then by plotting the distribution of that sample's individuals when the population is Normal, a graph with a shape like Figure 1.1 should result, and be quite close to a Normal.

A motoring analogy

Everyone knows that vehicle journey times are uncertain. On bad days, traffic suffers congestion, but on other days flows freely. Some days you catch all the traffic lights, most days catch a few, and on really lucky days they all work in your favor. The times taken for a given journey are unlikely to be exactly Normally distributed, because there can be too many 'extreme' outcomes from accidents, fallen trees, heavy snow, etc., blocking roads. Nevertheless, the assumption of Normality may serve as a good first approximation, helping to capture the inherent uncertainty. On any given day, a forecast of how long your journey will take may be reasonably accurate, but will be incorrect to some extent.

Lesson 1 in forecasting: future outcomes are uncertain, so even if very good forecasts are correct on average, they will usually be 'wrong' by some amount.

Let's think about the average speed of our journey. Figure 1.3 shows the time taken in hours to travel a given distance assuming a *constant* speed of 50 miles per hour (mph). The vertical axis records the distance traveled in miles at 50 mile intervals, starting at zero (which, of course, takes zero time). The horizontal axis shows how many hours such a distance would take to cover at 50 mph. The assumption of a constant speed ensures the relationship between distance and time is linear. The dotted lines show that traveling 200 miles would take 4 hours. Such a relationship can be used to 'forecast' how long a journey of a different distance would take under identical conditions, so 500 miles would be forecast to take 10 hours. Notice that the graph would look identical if both axes were relabeled in kilometers and kilometers per hour.

Unfortunately, although 'cruise control devices' would allow a constant speed to be set, the reality is that traffic rarely flows at a constant speed. Consequently, we need to combine the idea of a distribution of possible outcomes in Figure 1.2 with a graph like Figure 1.3. So we need

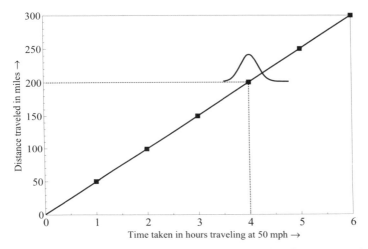

Figure 1.3: Illustrating a linear relation between the distance traveled at a constant speed and the time taken.

to think about the range of probable times for each journey of a given distance, say our example of 200 miles, when speeds vary around a target, say 50 mph. Now 4 hours becomes the center of a distribution of times to reach 200 miles, with a spread of say 40 minutes either side, corresponding to a fastest average speed of 60 mph and a slowest of just above 40 mph. This is illustrated by the small distribution with a longer right tail, showing a possible range of times, as the occasional rather longer times than the average are more likely than rather shorter.

Lesson 2 in forecasting: correctly measuring the forecast uncertainty is important.

Moreover, not all relations are linear as in Figure 1.3. To illustrate, Figure 1.4 shows the non-linear relation for the emergency stopping distance needed by a 'standard' car traveling at different speeds. The non-linearity arises from the different roles of the distance that physical braking needs to halt the vehicle, and the distance traveled during the time taken to real-ize that braking is urgently required. Notice that here the axes start at 20 mph and 40 feet: always read the units on both axes carefully!

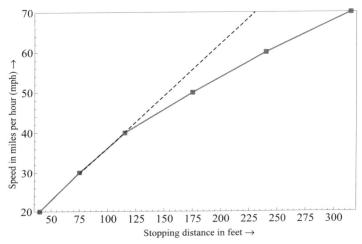

Figure 1.4: Stopping distances for a standard car traveling at different speeds.

Stopping distances almost double going from 20 mph to 30 mph. Like-wise, the stopping distance almost doubles again from 40 mph to 60 mph. The vertical axis only rises to 70 mph: at 100 mph, it would take about 500 feet to stop, twice the distance at 60 mph. The dashed straight line shows what a linear relation would predict. At 70 mph, the linear relation would predict that one could stop in 230 feet, not the 315 feet it would actually take even with an alert driver and good brakes. A bad accident could result if the linear relation is incorrectly assumed, albeit implicitly by the drivers involved.

Lesson 3 in forecasting: mistakes can occur if a linear model is incorrectly assumed when the relation is not linear.

An 'average speed' is *not* the arithmetic mean of the distribution of speeds during a journey. Imagine a 20 mile journey to work by car, where the first 10 miles are on a motorway, traveled at 60 mph, and the last 10 in London at 10 mph. The average speed is *not* $(60 + 10)/2 = 35$ mph. Rather the first part of the journey took 10 minutes, and the last part an hour, so the 20 miles were covered in 70 minutes which is just over 17 mph. Average journey speeds are most affected by the *slowest* speeds— because you spend more time there. Even if the first 10 miles had been traveled above the legal speed limit at say 100 mph, so took just 6 minutes, the average speed would be just over 18 mph, a small improvement at considerable risk. The longer right-hand 'tail' of the distribution shown in Figure 1.3 reflects the fact that slower speeds, such as from being stopped at traffic lights or in an accident, play a bigger role than faster speeds in determining average speed.

Lesson 4 in forecasting: mistakes can occur if the wrong statistical approach (here an arithmetic mean) is used to make the calculations (average journey speed).

In real life, we most certainly do not travel at a random sample of speeds around our target. Successive speeds for a given stage of the journey are likely to be similar, and possibly quite different from the speeds for other stages. If we wanted to forecast the final arrival time at work after (say) 15 miles had been traveled, we would need to use a model specifically designed for the second half, not one for the journey up to that point that combines motorway and urban speeds. In an important sense, the model has shifted after 10 miles, and that is germane to getting a forecast for the arrival time that is at all accurate.

Lesson 5 in forecasting: mistakes can occur if the data shift relative to the model.

Our car journey example has highlighted five aspects that are required for a usefully accurate forecast with an appropriate measure of its uncertainty. The correct form of the relation, an accurate measure of the forecast uncertainty, the correct model form, an appropriate statistical method, and the times at which a model shifts are all needed. Unfortunately, all five are usually unknown and need to be learnt from the available evidence. There are methods for doing so, although they involve statistical considerations, making the resulting forecasts less than perfectly reliable. Furthermore, these are not the only difficulties to be overcome, as shown below.

Beware false forecasting

Here is a charlatan's trick for you. Consider contacting 1024 investors, sending half of them the message that the price of shares in company X will rise in the next week and the other half that the price will fall. Whichever transpires, send half of the successful group of 512 the new message that shares in company Y will rise in the next week, and tell the other half that they will fall. Continue contacting the successfully-predicted group of 256 with similar tales about company Z, 128 about company W, and so on (64, 32, 16) till after six 'successful forecasts' you tell the remaining 8 that they will have to pay for such good advice in the future.

Although a somewhat far-fetched parable, some economists are famous for having forecast five of the last two recessions. But an important point is the difficulty in evaluating how good forecasts are when many are made, some of which may be contradictory. Indeed, beware of forecasts that are made frequently, cover many possibilities, and are somewhat ambiguous, followed by highlighting the few successes—although financiers may be forced to admit that 'past returns are not a reliable guide to future returns', they may still announce loudly that they were the best performing fund over some time period.

Time, models and the future

Forecasting requires looking into the future, that is, towards a time that has still to arrive, and perhaps also at a different place as on a journey. As noted above, we will only consider forecasting based on rules, which mainly comprise models estimated from past data, or time series. A time series is any set of observations ordered by the passing of time, so 1945 happened before 1946. The frequency of the time series is important, varying from very high (nanoseconds) through hourly, monthly to annual and longer, with many other frequencies in between. Frequency influences how far into the future anyone might sensibly forecast: it makes little sense to try and forecast an hourly outcome on a given day 5 years ahead. Weather forecasts often provide separate types of forecast for the next 24 hours, and the upcoming summer. We will consider many time series in this book, together with forecasts made at different points in time for various future dates. The recent M4 forecasting competition asked for forecasts over various horizons for 100,000 time series across a range of frequencies from hourly, through daily, weekly, monthly, to quarterly and annual.[8]

Figure 1.5 illustrates four very different time series. The first in Panel (a) shows atmospheric CO_2 levels over the last 800,000 years from 1000 year ice core measures, with Ice Ages and warmer interglacial periods at troughs and peaks respectively. Panel (b) records the annual percentage changes in the UK's National Debt since the founding of the Bank of England in 1694, where 'spikes' mainly coincide with wars till the 20th Century when major recessions also have an impact; (c) is the population of the UK in millions since 1875 recorded annually, but interpolated between censuses till relatively recently. Finally Panel (d) shows the daily prediction market probabilities of Mr Obama winning the presidential election in November 2009.

Consider attempting to forecast their future behavior. CO_2 levels rose dramatically after the Industrial Revolution, and are now above 400 ppm. This would have been completely unexpected based on the historical variation in the series, which saw levels ranging from highs of 300 to lows of 175 ppm. Imagine trying to forecast the changes in the National Debt even a year ahead—you would have had to forecast the starts and ends of wars! The population time series looks smooth, and on the face of it would seem to be easier to forecast. In part this is because the data are interpolated. Even so, there are dips and spurts which would have proven hard to

---

[8] M4 is the latest in a series of open competitions aimed at identifying 'the most accurate forecasting method(s) for different types of predictions': see https://www.m4.unic.ac.cy/.

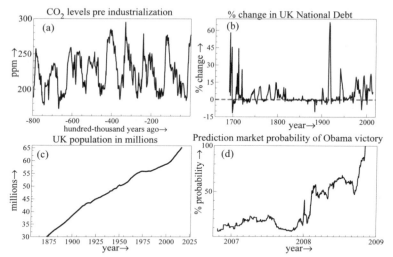

Figure 1.5: (a) Atmospheric CO_2 levels over the last 800,000 years in parts per million (ppm); (b) annual percentage changes in the UK's National Debt; (c) annual population of the UK in millions; (d) daily prediction market probabilities of an Obama presidential election victory in 2009.

anticipate without detailed knowledge of the social and economic forces shaping society. The last time series is a forecast, made at each point in time, reflecting the probability that Obama would be victorious. The forecast probability is very low at the start—given that the event in question occurred. The probability of an Obama win only stays permanently above 50% after mid-September 2009. Forecasting is hard, whether at the 1000 year time scale, or with daily-updated forecasts.

A forecasting model is a formalized description of the relationship between what we observe has happened in the past and what we then think may happen in the future. For example, the model may be as simple as forecasting that the annual population of the UK in 2019 might be $x\%$ higher than in 2018, where $x\%$ is the annual percentage increase in 2018 over 2017. This is essentially a forecast of 'more of the same', or a 'same again' forecast. Or $x\%$ might be the historical average increase over the last century. Either way, the 'model' captures the observed tendency of the population to grow. A more sophisticated model would result if it were possible to forecast the birth and death rates based on socio-economic trends and the age-profile of the population. Forecasting models can be relatively simple, or large and complicated, like those used at many central banks and international agencies.

Most of this book can be understood without our explicitly describing the details of the models being used for forecasting or how they were developed. However, a few basic properties of almost all such models will be explained as we proceed, placed in boxes to highlight that they are somewhat more technical, but not essential to understanding the text explanations.

The road ahead—literally

'Forecasters have sometimes described their task as similar to driving in a thick fog using only the rear-view mirror, but I think that is an understatement. To make the metaphor more exact, add misted windows, an unreliable clutch, a blindfold, and handcuffs, not to mention the unsignposted cliff a hundred meters down the road.'
Diane Coyle, 'Making sense of published economic forecasts' in Hendry and Neil Ericsson, *Understanding Economic Forecasts*, MIT Press, 2001.

The task facing the economic forecaster was likened by Coyle to a motorist on a road trip. Throughout this book, we will extend her analogy to the apparently simple problem of forecasting the journey time by car to a given destination that is traveled regularly by the motorist in question. And we will discuss in what ways forecasters can try and load the dice in their favor.

Chapter 2

How do we make forecasts?

Prophecy is a good line of business, but it is full of risks.
Mark Twain, *Following the Equator: A Journey Around the World*, Hartford: American Publishing Co., 1897.

This chapter first discusses the large number of words in English that relate to 'seeing into the future', and their associated methods of forecasting. We then consider how our motorist might forecast her journey times. More uncertainty is added to her journey-time forecast by introducing what happens when 'unforeseen' obstructions occur, although she could try updating her forecasts as time goes by and information accrues. We also reveal that apparent uncertainty, as measured by the forecaster, can differ from the actual uncertainty that obtains in the real situation.

A galaxy of terms, and ways, for 'seeing into the future'

Most readers will know some synonyms for forecasting, such as 'predicting', and most Thesauruses will list a small number of possibilities. In fact, there are at least 30 words in English relevant to 'looking into the future', including, in alphabetic order:

anticipate (as children do with gifts before their birthdays);

augury (using signs, usually based on animal behavior);

Cassandra (correctly seeing into the future, but not being believed);

clairvoyant (seeing things not present to the senses);

conjecture (a claim not well based on evidence);

Delphic (an ambiguous statement about future events, believed to have been obtained under a trance);

divination (with divine or occult help);

expectation (a view of the future, common in economic theories);

extrapolate (extend a current trend into the future);

foreboding; foreknowledge; foreseeing; foreshadowing; foretelling; forewarning (somewhat sinister views of what will come to pass);

omen (sign of a future event);

oracle (forecasting based on a claim to 'higher' powers);

portend (warn in advance);

precognition (know before the occurrence);

premonition (sense a future event);

presage (indication of a yet-to-happen event);

prescience (foreknowledge);

prognosis (often used to describe the likely future development of an illness);

project (extend into the future);

prophecy (to claim certain knowledge of a future outcome, usually with divine help)

scry (to practice crystal-ball gazing);

seer (one who sees into the future); and

soothsaying (claiming to have supernatural insight of the future).

Many of these words are associated with methods of forecasting used in the past, now usually discredited (such as dreams; tea leaves; animal entrails; comets in the sky and eclipses warning of doom, etc.).[1] In the course of time, they have acquired disreputable connotations. Others have yet to acquire adverse meanings, but may need to change the name of their activity once that happens. In the public's view, economic forecasting does not currently have a high reputation. It was famously claimed that economic forecasting was 'invented to make weather forecasters look good'. Another central aim of this book is to explain the general difficulties of forecasting in a turbulent world, even for such a mundane matter as a road trip.

Many dictionaries consider 'forecast' and 'predict' to be close alternatives, but we will use them in rather different senses, more like common usage for a weather forecast, but not a weather prediction. The word 'predict' concerns an inference from established laws of nature: for example, Albert Einstein predicted that light waves would be bent by the gravitational field of the sun, and was an instant celebrity when in May 1919 Sir Arthur Eddington established that was correct. Whether or not an event is predictable is a property of that event, irrespective of our ability to actually predict it. Conversely, a 'forecast' is surrounded by greater uncertainty. As an example, consider the imminent arrival of Captain James Cook approaching New Zealand on October 6, 1769. He was exploring the Pacific ocean looking for new lands, but did not know that an island lay ahead.

---

[1]Cassandra remains relevant for UK economists whose forecasts were condemned by Michael Gove, former Justice Secretary in the UK Government.

The Māori were unaware that Cook's ship, the *Endeavour*, was approaching, and, at that time, their language had no words for many of the devices it carried, such as cannons. But take a step back: to a person on the Moon with a sufficiently powerful telescope watching the path of the *Endeavour*, the meeting was completely predictable.

Making forecasts

Events are always forecastable, since a forecast is any statement about the future, but nothing guarantees the outcome will be near the forecast. One may even try to forecast an unpredictable event, albeit usually unsuccessfully. However, the forecasts of interest here are those made by formal devices or methods, which we call 'forecasting rules' with replicable outcomes. Nevertheless, there are two basic methods of forecasting:

(1) By a 'crystal ball', time machine, or an equivalent, that can genuinely 'see' into the future;

(2) by extrapolating from present information.

Unfortunately, as expressed by Robert J. Samuelson, *Washington Post*, June 16, 2001: 'Never a crystal ball when you need one'. Because working examples of (1) seem unavailable to humanity, we are forced to focus on the dramatically inferior method (2) for 'forecasting'. The success of any forecasting device, method or approach requires that:

(a) there are regularities to be captured;

(b) those regularities are informative about the future;

(c) the proposed method captures such regularities; yet

(d) excludes distorting non-regularities (noise).

(a) and (b) are properties of whatever one is trying to forecast, so, although essential, are out of the control of the forecaster, whereas (c) and (d) are properties of the proposed forecasting method, so are open to analysis and possible improvement. There do seem to be many regularities in life—today is a lot like yesterday—but some things have changed, sometimes abruptly. It is the latter that prevent forecasting from being easy even when processes appear to be persistent. Consequently, achieving (c) without violating (d) is difficult. For example, including lots of influences in a forecasting device may ensure it captures any regularities, but also makes it likely that irregularities which can suddenly shift are also included. The balance between these determines which forecasting methods will be successful in practice.

Widely used forecasting methods include:

- Guessing, which only requires luck, so may seem risky, but has fewest assumptions.

- 'Rules of thumb' need an intuitive 'feel' for the behavior of whatever is being forecast, sometimes referred to as flying by the seat of your pants, whereas it seems preferable to fly by your brain.

- Naive extrapolation merely needs the present trends to continue, but we will shortly see the consequence for forecasting of that assumption failing.

- 'Leading indicators' require that what led yesterday will still lead today, but we all know of sporting teams well ahead at one point that eventually lose.

- Surveys of intentions and expectations require that the individuals surveyed correctly reveal their plans, but mis-predictions of election and referendum outcomes suggest that is not always the case.

- Simple models require that the process to be forecast is relatively regular contrary to the evidence of intermittent abrupt, or very rapid, change.

- Formal forecasting systems require rather a lot of assumptions, and can go badly awry, but they consolidate knowledge in progressive research, and can help to explain their own failures.

Forecasting her journey time

Our motorist's first calculations of her estimated time of arrival (ETA) were probably based on a map of the potential journey, although she might also receive useful information from other sources, such as the traffic news on the radio, as well as real-time information from electronic devices about stationary and slow-moving traffic on her planned route. Consider just the map for now. A road map is a *model* of the road network which connects the motorist's starting point and destination. It schematically represents connections between locations. However, it is incomplete for the purpose at hand (namely calculating her ETA), because, although it might accurately indicate distances between locations, it typically will not give the *average* speeds that one might expect to achieve on different stretches, and certainly not the *actual* speeds at which the motorist will progress. So an exact calculation of journey time will not be possible. Nevertheless, maps that accurately portray *connections* are invaluable when planning a trip.

The economic equivalent of a road map is a model of the economy. Such models seek to embody our best knowledge of the linkages in an economy, to capture how current economic conditions will evolve over time and determine the future state of the economy. Evaluating a map's accuracy involves checking whether or not the roads really do link up as marked on the map. At one level, evaluating an econometric model is similar, but is not so easy in practice. What we'd like to do is hold everything in the model fixed and manipulate one input at a time, measuring its effect on the output. This enables us to assess whether the model's prediction that a change in X will give rise to a change of a given magnitude in Y holds in the real world. But this is not possible in a largely non-experimental, observational science such as macroeconomics. Holding everything else fixed is out of the question. Historically there will have been times when X changed, but typically many other potentially confounding factors will also have occurred, so that deciding whether it is a good model or not is far from trivial.

Maps are designed for different purposes: compare a street map of London showing the relative positions of Westminster Cathedral and St.

Pauls Cathedral, with a map of their underground stations designed to clarify connections. Maps can also be on the wrong scale, with too much—or too little—detail, or both. For example, a tourist map might helpfully offer a 3D impression of buildings, but fail to record which roads are one-way only. Moreover, a map of the main road routes of England designed to show how someone arriving at the Channel ports can journey to Scotland bypassing London altogether would be needlessly cluttered if the main tourist sights of London were shown. The motorist's map and the economist's model are more fundamentally different in that road maps are essentially scale models of the road network, whereas economic models are stylized mathematical descriptions of the economy in the form of systems of linked relationships. Actually, one of the earliest models of the economy, the 'Phillips machine' or MONIAC, was a hydraulic model. In *A Few Hares to Chase*, Oxford University Press, 2016, Alan Bollard provides a wonderful biography of Bill Phillips' amazing life, from a prisoner of war to an economics professor without a degree, including a description of MONIAC and its construction, a working version of which still resides in the Reserve Bank of New Zealand.

Nevertheless, just as maps are designed for particular purposes, which determine the scale at which the map is drawn, so economists' forecasting models need to be fit for purpose: models built to describe or understand an economy might not work well for forecasting future outcomes.

Forecasting in 'normal' times

In normal circumstances, the motorist's estimate based on the road map and traffic reports, etc., will be sufficiently accurate to ensure arrival at the destination at roughly the anticipated time. On any particular journey, however, many small factors will cause variations in actual journey times around that estimate: bad luck in being stopped at a sequence of traffic lights, or heavier traffic than usual, and so on. If our motorist is undertaking a similar journey on a number of occasions (e.g., commuting), then we can calculate the variability around the average journey time. One measure of this variability is the *variance* of the forecast error, where the forecast error is the difference between the actual time of arrival (ATA) and the estimate (namely ATA minus ETA). Often it is more useful to calculate the square root of the variance, which is the forecast-error standard deviation. This particular measure—the forecast-error standard deviation—can be most easily understood when expressed as a percentage of the average journey time. A large value, such as 50%, denotes an unreliable route, where a journey may well take between one-and-a-half times and half as long as expected. A small value, say 5%, is what most motorists would like, to ensure arrival within roughly $[-3, +3]$ (usually denoted ± 3) minutes on a journey of about an hour.

Similarly, with economic forecasts, there will be a number of intervening factors which entail that the forecast value will typically not equal the actual value. This is to be expected both because economic data are imprecise, and economic models are not exact. By this we mean that the relations determining the various outcomes such as gross domestic product (GDP, the total of what is produced within a country) and inflation have random error terms which are not forecastable. You can think of these as a measure of the modeler's ignorance. The variability of the random error terms goes a long way to determining the forecast-error standard deviation in normal times. As in the motoring example, a large percentage standard deviation for a forecast entails an imprecise forecast.

Now consider forecasting GDP, usually taken as 'the' measure of an economy's level of output. Many factors influence its value, such as consumers' spending, company investment, government spending decisions, and exports, so errors are inevitable. Inflation forecasts will also depend on a multitude of inter-related factors, including wage agreements, prices of raw materials and energy, the exchange rate, the level of demand in the economy, and so on. Again, errors are inevitable, but we can use a distribution like that in Figure 1.2 to approximate the behavior of such errors. For example, if the error terms can be assumed to be (approximately at least) drawings from a Normal distribution with a mean of zero and a standard deviation of s, say, then we know that 95% of the time the error term will lie in the interval $-2s$, $+2s$. Because the error term is the difference between past actual values and how well, or poorly, our model previously fitted, we can estimate how it might fare when used for forecasting.

An important point is that we don't require either that the map is a 100% faithful representation of the road network or that the economist's model is a perfect representation of the economy in order to obtain reasonable forecasts. The road map may be out of date. Some roads shown on the map may no longer exist, so that some journeys may come to a temporary termination in a dead-end. But the motorist may simply be able to retrace her steps and find another road going in the appropriate direction without causing undue delay—and avoid the non-existent route on future journeys. Provided none of the map-induced errors in the route taken by the motorist are catastrophic, and can be resolved with short detours and occasional back-tracking, then the motorist would come to know that journey times typically took, say, 10% longer than her best estimate based on her map (and her other sources of information), so later forecasts of journey times could be adjusted accordingly, being increased by 10%.

The same is true of economic forecasting. Modern economies are so complicated that no one could hope for 'correct' road maps thereof: models are virtually bound to incorrectly omit important linkages that are not known, and unknowingly include ones that are irrelevant. This class of problems is called model mis-specification, and it adds to a forecaster's difficulties. In particular, model mis-specification complicates calculating the likely magnitudes of forecast errors, and usually increases the variance of the resulting forecast errors. Sometimes, no substantial problems ensue, as when non-existent roads are not part of the route, or the missing linkage is not involved in the forecast. At other times, the effects may be more serious, such as ending up at a non-existent bridge or in a field with no alternative route! However, provided the model mis-specification does not systematically mislead the forecaster, model mis-specification of itself may not be problematic to the forecasts of our motorist or an economist.

More uncertainty

Motorists are well aware that unexpected events can upset the most carefully laid plans. And of course the occurrence of such events, and their consequences in terms of tiring and fraught journeys, are likely to color people's perceptions and be remembered. A pothole that punctures a tire, or worse breaks an axle, a crash in the traffic ahead, or unexpectedly bad weather all can create an extended delay, as can more extreme events, such as a bridge collapsing or an earthquake. These events occur intermittently. They can be viewed as rare realizations from a set of adverse factors. Effectively, when such a bad event happens, the mean of the journey time has been shifted from its norm to a much larger value, so that the actual journey time in such instances is likely to be much larger than journey times hitherto. However, some of these effects are transient, albeit annoying, such as a puncture where a tire can be changed relatively speedily, whereas others have longer-lasting effects, such as an unusable bridge which might take months to repair. Such persistent outcomes are called *location shifts*, as they change the level of the journey time, or economic outcome.

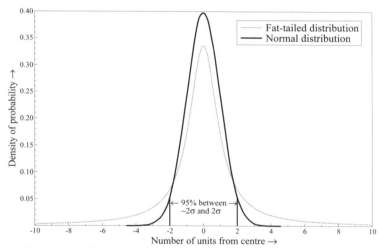

Figure 2.1: Illustrating increased uncertainty about journey delays.

Unexpectedly long, but transient, delays can be described by the dotted distribution plotted in Figure 2.1. First, the solid distribution is the Normal distribution, like that plotted in Figure 1.2. The dotted distribution has a lower peak, and spreads out more along the horizontal axis. This is known as a fat-tailed distribution, and has a much greater chance of a random draw occurring at, say, -8 or +9, than the Normal distribution. A puncture due to a pothole causes a journey delay well outside of the Normal distribution. It was an unexpected event. But its possible occurrence can be characterized by the dotted distribution as it allows for a much wider uncertainty around the average journey delay of zero. Similar problems face economic forecasters when a large shock hits an economy, say a sudden dock strike or a sharp fall in its main stock market, but is rapidly resolved or quickly rebounds, so only has a transient effect.

However, if an alternative route, or resolution, is not available, or the severity of the problem and ongoing delays ahead are not recognized, forecast errors may be both large and persistent, forcing the motorist to update her ETA dramatically as time passes. Forecast failure is said to occur when, as here, forecasts are much less accurate than expected based on previous experience. The parallel in economics defines forecast failure as occurring when the forecasts are much less accurate than the past forecast performance of the model. Of course, positive events can also occur: a slow section of roadworks ends, or a new bypass round a congested city is opened early. If the event causes a permanent shift in the average journey time, such as a new bypass or a collapsed bridge, there is a *systematic* location shift, so needs to be taken into account in future journeys.

Permanent shifts in journey times, or the levels of GDP, are not well described by the distributions in Figure 2.1. With random sampling, the expected journey time is just as likely to be much shorter as much longer under the dotted distribution. Such distributions describe one-off events, such as a punctured tire, but not a new bypass, a collapsed bridge or the impact on GDP of a major war. Now take a look at Figure 2.2.

We have added a further distribution to those shown in Figure 2.1, namely the distribution shown by dashed lines. This is just another Normal distribution (in solid) that has been shifted up to be centered at a delay of 5 hours, the increased time the detour will take to reach the other side of the river. The collapsed bridge means that future journey delays will be longer than they have been in the past. So, when using that route from now on, expected journey delays should be calculated by using the dashed

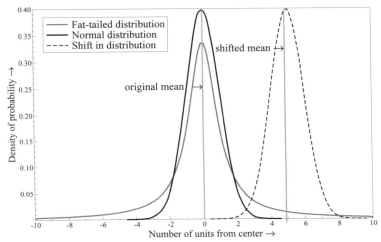

Figure 2.2: Illustrating a jump in journey delays.

distribution, not the original one. The most likely outcome for this distribution is 5 hours longer, with its associated uncertainty. If our motorist uses the solid or dotted distributions to forecast her ETA after a location shift, she will continue to observe forecast failure.

In economics, the analog of an unexpected event such as a collapsed bridge also happens. The Financial Crisis is one example from many. Such events are key to understanding why systematic forecast failure occurs. Because they shift the location (mean) of the variable (journey time in the motoring example, perhaps the rate of inflation in economics) from one value (the previous norm) to another (after the adverse event), then the new value persists. Economic history reveals the occurrence of numerous economic 'collapsed bridges', leading to high unemployment, major falls in GDP, large rises in inflations etc. Possible remedies for systematic forecast errors due to location shifts will be an important preoccupation of the rest of this book.

Illustrating forecast uncertainty

So far, we have not presented any actual forecasts, so let us start down that road. The graph in Figure 2.3 shows UK 'narrow money', called M1, which is essentially all cash and coin in circulation plus all money held in checking accounts. Here money is measured in constant prices to show its purchasing power over time. To calculate a constant price time series requires a measure of aggregate prices, where we have used the price index for total expenditure in the UK, since M1 money is mainly used for spending. Then each observation on the total amount of actual money in M1 is divided by that price.

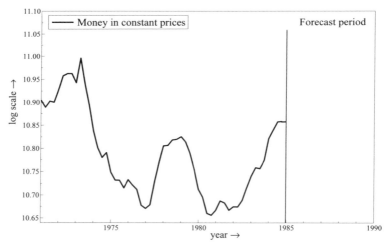

Figure 2.3: UK narrow money in constant prices.

The resulting units in which constant-price M1 is measured then depend on how the price index is defined: this could be 1.0 in 1965, or 100 in 1980, and so on. Fortunately, those particular units do not matter after taking logarithms as the scale becomes an additive constant. Consequently, Figure 2.3 reports the logs of the time series.

As the vertical scale on the graph is in logarithms, going from say 10.9 to 11.0 (as happens at the start) is a 10% increase, and returning to 10.9 is a 10% fall. The log-change is symmetric. However, when a shop raises a price from say £10 to £11, it quotes a price increase of 10%, but now cutting the price by 10% reduces it to £9.90—so it is not symmetric. The horizontal axis is time, but only 5-year markers are shown. The data are in fact quarterly observations that have been seasonally adjusted, so the very large rises around Decembers are 'removed' to let us 'see' the more general shape over time. After a brief rise initially, there is a steady drop till 1977, a 'bump' till early 1980, then a marked rise starting again in mid-1982. The last observation shown is 1984:Q4, denoting the fourth quarter of 1984, where the time series has leveled off.

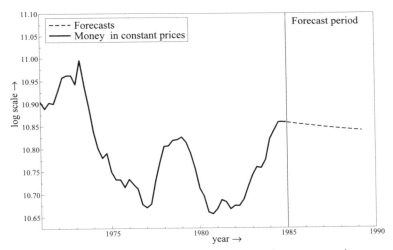

Figure 2.4: Forecasts for UK narrow money in constant prices.

Now consider Figure 2.4. Behind the scenes, we have built a model to explain how much money is likely to be held in the UK. The details of that model need not concern us here, but total expenditure, its rate of inflation, and interest rates all play a role in how much money the British are willing to hold: more as incomes rise (as people tend to spend more), but less as higher inflation erodes the value of money or as interest rates rise.

As we do not know the future values of those variables, they have to be forecast as well, which we have done in order to produce the forecasts of constant-price money through to 1989:Q2. The resulting forecasts are shown by the dashed line, which declines slowly. This is the net effect of rising incomes inducing more money to be held, offset by forecasts of continuing high inflation and interest rates. Forecasts like these for constant-price money are called 'point' forecasts and convey an impression of precision and certainty. The apparent certainty is unwarranted—many events could happen over the next five years!

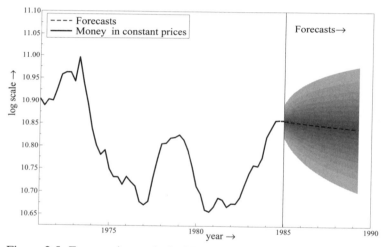

Figure 2.5: Forecast intervals for UK narrow money in constant prices.

Figure 2.5 seeks to address the false security of a straight-line forecast by plotting a 'fan chart' of uncertainty around the forecast. Such fan charts were pioneered by the Bank of England, and the uncertainty is reflected in the lightness of the fan lines: dark lines mark a likely interval, faint lines show rather less likely outcomes. Think of a sequence of Normal distributions (discussed in Chapter 1) rising vertically out of the figure towards you at each observation, centered on the dashed line where the span of the fan covers 95% of the distribution.

The fans open out more the further ahead to account for more random shocks occurring over longer time intervals. For the last forecast, the fan spans a range of more than 25% of the money stock, so that forecast is highly uncertain. Forecasters often provide interval forecasts as in Figure 2.5, showing a range within which they anticipate the outcome will lie, and these can be reported in many ways, some of which will be used in later chapters, including both uncertainty bars and bands around forecasts.

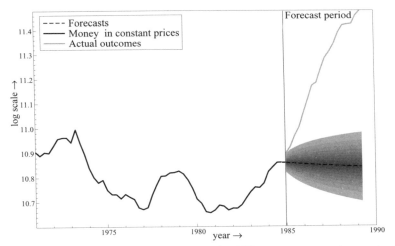

Figure 2.6: Forecasts with the outturns for UK narrow money in constant prices.

Finally, Figure 2.6 adds the outcomes for money holdings that actually occurred over the forecast horizon 1984:Q4–1989:Q2, shown as a dotted line. *The forecasts are wildly wrong*, going in the wrong direction and being dramatically too low! This is an example of forecast failure: the observations lie well outside what was thought to be a reasonable range.

Notice that the new data rise far higher than any previous observations, dwarfing earlier values: it cannot be a surprise that it is difficult to forecast outcomes that lie well outside the historical experience. Nevertheless, what explains such a spectacular mis-forecast? Is it a bad model, or were the forecasts of expenditure, inflation and interest rates poor, or something else?

In fact, in the Finance Act of 1984, commercial banks were ordered to deduct income tax from the interest payments they made on savings accounts, and transfer those tax revenues to the Tax Authority (then called the Inland Revenue). It was (correctly) believed by the Government that many recipients of interest income did not declare them for tax purposes, so to avoid being caught after this change, evaders shifted money out of savings deposits into checking accounts. To 'compensate' savers for that move, commercial banks started offering substantial interest rates on checking accounts—leading to a huge inflow of money. The poor forecaster in 1984:Q2 could not have foreseen a shift to paying interest rates in double figures on checking accounts when previously they had been zero, so failed to allow for the huge increase in the money measure they were trying to forecast.

Adapting to forecast failure

Do not despair. Despite this debacle, such prolonged and huge failures almost never occur in practice. Soon after forecasts start to go awry, forecasters will adjust their models (in ways explained later). Here that proved to be straightforward—appropriately allowing for the high interest rates that checking accounts were paying after 1985:Q1. In essence, the previous model correctly assumed that zero interest was paid on such accounts, so the competitive rate measure was what savers could earn elsewhere. But, after the Act, the differential between that competitive rate and the interest on checking accounts is what mattered. To adjust for that major shift, replace the previous interest rate in the model by the differential, keeping everything else the same. That is essentially all that is needed to produce the forecasts shown in Figure 2.7.[2] However, to dramatize the difference from Figure 2.6, we have used the actual later outcomes for income, inflation and interest rates: so please persevere!

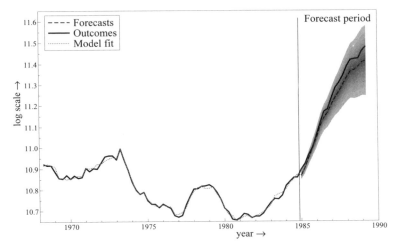

Figure 2.7: Forecasts with the outturns for UK narrow money in constant prices after adjusting the measures of interest rates.

There are two important points to note. First, exactly the same model is used to forecast in Figures 2.6 and 2.7! The only difference is what measures of interest rates are used in the forecasts, namely redefining the opportunity cost of holding M1 once it earned interest. Second, the reason the data stop at 1989:Q2 is that M1 then ceased to be meaningful when several large UK building societies (rather like US savings and loans associations) converted to being commercial banks. Doing so meant their huge short-term deposits, which in effect were checking accounts, went from outside M1 to being a component, leading to large jumps in the measured

---

[2] In fact, it took time for people to react to this change, so the model needed a 'learning adjustment' to the interest rate differential.

series. Again, that is 'just' a change of definition, but it greatly altered the relationship between measured M1 and other economic variables such as inflation, although there was no actual impact from the reclassification, thereby at last establishing the irrelevance of measured M1 for economic policies.

Updating forecasts as time goes by

Our motorist can update her ETA as the journey progresses, just as an economic forecaster may make several forecasts of, say, UK narrow money in 1989:Q2, the last quarter shown in Figure 2.6. That figure shows forecasts made using information through 1984:Q3. The 1989:Q2 value could also be forecast using information through 1988:Q2—this would be a one-year ahead forecast. Or even using a dataset up to and including 1989:Q1, which would be a one-quarter ahead forecast, and so on. Just as one might expect the motorist's ETA would get closer to her actual time of arrival (ATA) as the journey progresses, so one might expect the economist's forecast of narrow money in 1989:Q2 would get closer to the value that will actually occur as the length of the horizon diminishes. Indeed, the only unknown value underlying the first forecast for the amount of money that will be held in 1985:Q1 in Figure 2.7 is the random shock, hence its relatively high accuracy. The remarkable accuracy over the next few years is partly due to luck, as only small shocks perturbed the relation till 1989:Q2 when a further massive shift occurred.

For the motorist, there remain fewer possible unknown future 'events' that can go wrong as the journey progresses: as she turns into the correct street and sees her destination, her forecast of arriving in the next half-minute is likely to be fulfilled unless thwarted by mechanical failure, or running out of petrol, etc. Arguing by analogy, it seems reasonable to expect short-horizon economic forecasts to be more accurate than long-horizon forecasts. In our money example, the forecaster will observe ever more of the steep rise in money holdings as the forecast origin moves beyond 1984:Q4, and using that information might improve accuracy dramatically compared to Figure 2.6. Indeed that happened in reality. But even in 'normal times', forecast accuracy should be better at shorter horizons, as less can go wrong.

Of course, short-horizon forecasts may not be so valuable to either the motorist or economist: as the motorist pulls up outside her destination, the value of a phone call informing the inhabitants of her arrival may be less useful than an accurate forecast communicated to the inhabitants an hour or so before her arrival. In the economics arena, a one-month ahead forecast that inflation looks set to exceed the Chancellor's target may not be very helpful if the economy is known to respond slowly to monetary policy levers. We return below to an assessment of the value of a forecast in terms of the purpose for which it is made.

Sources of information

Many factors will influence journey time. Apart from the distance to be driven, these factors include the type of car, the type of road and its quality, the driver's skill (and personality), the traffic density, the time of day for traveling, the weather, and whether the journey takes in border controls or ferry crossings, *inter alia*. The motorist factors these in as best she can, and uses any additional available information, such as weather forecasts, and traffic reports, to arrive at an initial estimate of the trip's duration.

The economist also has a number of sources of information to inform any forecast. There are typically many models generating forecasts, as well as survey-based information on companies intentions, consumer expectations and sentiment, the views of financial markets, informed investors, and other 'experts'. Often combinations of forecasts from various sources improve forecast accuracy. This is obvious in the case of the motorist. The map provides information on distance, and a real-time traffic information service may provide information on the speed the traffic is moving at. These two pieces of information can be combined to provide a more accurate estimate of journey time than the map alone would provide, especially if traffic is flowing more slowly than normal.

We will consider the importance of information for economic forecasting in subsequent chapters. In economics, timely information about the current state of the economy is often crucial to forecasting the future accurately. However, as we explain in the next chapter, this type of information is not always readily available: unfortunately, in economics the present, and not just the future, is uncertain.

Chapter 3

Where are we before we forecast?

'You're travelling the wrong way.'
Train guard to Alice in Lewis Carroll, *Through the Looking-Glass and What Alice Found There*, London: Macmillan and Co., 1899.

The motorist and the economist

To plan her route before setting off on her journey, our motorist will want to locate her current position on her road map. She will also obviously need to know her destination, so that she knows where she is going—which may be a new location—and of course to know when she has arrived there. She may be unsure of her current position if the map does not provide enough detail, and perhaps omits some minor roads, so her exact starting point may only become clear as her journey progresses and she can understand the lie of the land.

Just as the motorist may have difficulty locating her starting point on the map, the economist's attempts to forecast the future may have to be grounded on a poor reading of the initial state of the economy. Many of the national accounts measures of the current level of activity are produced with delay and subject to revision. If we are interested in the total value of output that the economy is producing, we must look to official statistics on gross domestic product (GDP). It is often the yardstick for economic performance, and usually measures the level of economic activity over a three month period. But such estimates are released with a delay of more than a month, and even then are based on partial information that will almost certainly be revised. As time passes, more accurate estimates of GDP for the given quarter will be released, and in the fullness of time it might become apparent that the actual state of the economy was very different than appeared to be the case at the time. Both the motorist and the economist will have made their forecasts based on imperfect information about the starting point. In the late 1950s, British prime minister Harold MacMillan called basing policy on economic data like using 'last-year's Bradshaw' to catch trains, a reference to the famous railway timetable and guide initiated by George Bradshaw that helped popularize passenger travel in the mid-19th Century.

Equally, the end point may be uncertain. Suppose the motorist's destination is not precisely known by her. She knows the village her friend lives in, but not where her friend lives in the village, and there are no street names, still less house numbers. She has correctly forecast the time it will take to reach the village, but whether or not her overall journey-time forecast turns out to be accurate depends on whether she serendipitously happens across her friend's home, or has to stop and ask at a local shop. If the economist were attempting to forecast GDP, then revisions to the actual value may turn what at first appeared to be a good forecast into a poor forecast, or vice versa. For both motorist and economist the accuracy of the forecast may depend on how the 'outcome' is defined: arrival at her friend's village or her house; or the first or one of a later revised estimate of GDP.

> Diane Coyle also used to award the 'Golden Guru' prize for
> the most accurate UK macroeconomic forecasts of the 'mis-
> ery index', which was a combination of the rates of inflation

and unemployment, and GDP growth. She noted that the result depended on precisely when the outcomes were measured: even slight revisions would have changed the winner.

Why are data subject to revision? And why might it matter?

The forecaster's job is difficult enough, but is made all the harder by data being revised, so that we may only learn the correct values of today's key macroeconomic variables sometime in the future. Any forecast is contingent on the data available at the time: a bad starting point will usually worsen the forecast accuracy. Imagine our poor driver has been taken blindfold to an unknown road and has no compass, so only gradually gets her bearings as she begins to drive towards her desired destination—a longer trip will result.

Government statistics agencies, such as the Bureau of Economic Analysis (BEA) in the US, and the Office of National Statistics (ONS) in the UK, seek to provide timely statistics on key economic indicators concerning the current state of the economy. For example, the BEA publishes its first or 'advance' estimates of quarterly national accounts data about a month after the quarter in question. Notwithstanding the one month delay, these estimates are still only based on partial data sources. The estimates are then revised twice more at monthly intervals as more data become available and a more complete picture of the economy emerges. However, this is not the end of it. Substantial revisions are still possible during annual rounds of revisions for the next three years, and there are periodic comprehensive or benchmark revisions to incorporate methodological and conceptual improvements every five years or so. The ONS used to release its preliminary estimate of GDP 26–27 days after the quarter of interest, with a second estimate released with a lag of approximately 53 days, and the third estimate of GDP, the one which enters the Quarterly National Accounts, released 3 months after the end of the quarter. Historically, the delays in releasing estimates of GDP have been longer. This leads to an ever-changing baseline from which forecasts are made, and later evaluated.[1] In July 2018, the ONS started releasing rolling monthly and 3-monthly estimates of GDP, the first being for May. The new methodology uses output gross value added, with estimates of GDP updated later once more information on income and expenditure has accrued.

Let's have a look at some examples of these revisions for US real GDP.[2] The 2008–9 recession is a period when timely information on the current state of the economy would have been especially valuable to policy makers. In Table 3.1 as of July 2018, we can see that the US economy shrank by 2.7% in the first quarter of 2008. At the time, the first estimate suggested growth of 0.6%, similar to that in the fourth quarter of 2007. However, any fears that a recession loomed night have been allayed by the second estimate for 2008:Q1 (made towards the end of May), when growth was revised up to 0.9%, and yet higher in the third estimate. Policy-makers and forecasters are likely to have been wrong-footed by the difference between the original reading of the state of the economy in the first quarter of 2008 and that available 10 years later: in fact, the estimate of the output drop in 2008:Q1 was only revised down to near its 'final' value in August 2013, almost 5 years later, highlighted in bold.

Table 3.1: Entering the Great Recession

Release:	First	Second	Third	Most Recent
2007:Q4	0.64%	0.63%	0.58%	1.44%
2008:Q1	**0.60%**	**0.90%**	**0.96%**	**−2.70%**
2008:Q2	1.89%	3.28%	2.83%	2.00%

The contemporaneous reading of the current state of the economy as it entered the 'Great Recession' first went negative in 2008:Q3, with a first

---

[1] See https://www.ons.gov.uk/economy/grossdomesticproductgdp/bulletins/gdpmonthlyestimateuk/may2018.

[2] The data were downloaded from the Federal Reserve Bank of Philadelphia web site https://www.philadelphiafed.org/research-and-data/real-time-center/real-time-data/. The quarter-on-quarter rates in the table are expressed at annual rates (i.e., annualized percentage points).

estimate of -0.25%, followed by a decline of -3.8% in 2008:Q4, but both of these estimates proved to be hopelessly optimistic as Table 3.2 shows.

Table 3.2: Into the Great Recession

Release:	First	Second	Third	Most Recent
2008:Q3	-0.25%	-0.51%	-0.51%	-1.91%
2008:Q4	-3.80%	-6.25%	-6.34%	-8.19%

One might suspect that data revisions will be particularly large during recessions, or at turning points in the business cycle more generally, but there are examples of large revisions during normal times too. As an example, consider 2011:Q3 and 2011:Q4, with similar first estimates of around $2\frac{1}{2}$ to $2\frac{3}{4}\%$ growth. The first of these was revised down to 0.8%, and the second up to 4.6% as in Table 3.3.

Table 3.3: Other large revisions

Release:	First	Second	Third	Most Recent
2011:Q3	2.46%	2.00%	1.82%	0.84%
2011:Q4	2.75%	2.98%	2.96%	4.58%

The differences between these numbers are not small. Continual growth at 0.84% per annum would mean that real GDP doubled in about 86 years, compared to more than 40-fold over that time at a growth rate of 4.6%.

It is apparent that a forecaster who expects 'business as usual' and forecasts next quarter's growth rate to be equal to the current quarter's rate would have made very different forecasts depending on whether he or she used an early estimate of growth or, infeasibly, the value available a number of years later. It is not just seemingly naive 'business as usual' forecasters whose forecasts might be very wrong because the then-available estimate is very different from the 'truth'. All forecasts which start from the current (mis-measured) state of the economy are subject to such errors.

Before considering data revisions and forecasting further, the reader might wonder about the impact of data revisions on research in macroeconomics more generally. Dean Croushore and Tom Stark ask precisely this question: 'Does the data vintage matter?', where the vintage refers to a specific release of data for a given period.[3] They consider whether some influential findings in the literature are robust to data revisions, i.e., are the results qualitatively affected if, instead of using the original data vintage, a subsequent vintage of the data (covering the same historical period) is used instead? They find that some macroeconomic results are sensitive to the data vintage used. In our analogy, not only is our driver uncertain of her starting point, but her map will change in uncertain ways as information accrues—a new motorway is opened, or a bridge closed.

Forecasting data revisions

A natural question to ask in a book about forecasting is whether the data revisions—the differences between the earlier and later estimates—are themselves predictable. If the revisions were perfectly predictable at the time the first estimate was made, then one might think it odd for the agency not to release the revised estimate as the first. If there was some predictability in revisions, then our driver may have a better chance of navigating her way from the blind location she is commencing her journey from. To answer this question, forecasters distinguish between '*news*' and '*noise*'. The *news* may be in the form of a roadsign directing the driver to the motorway, and the *noise* could be a faulty compass that is affected by a rogue magnet.

Data revisions are said to be *news* if the revision (equivalently, the later estimate) cannot be predicted from the first estimate. Such revisions add genuinely new information. Alternatively, data revisions are said to be *noise* when they can be predicted. This is a useful distinction. However, revisions may be predictable using a wider information set consisting of related variables and other sources of information. Hence the finding that revisions are news, narrowly defined using only past data, does not tell us whether or not revisions are predictable. This is an important issue, because the problems associated with data revisions would be attenuated

---

[3]See Croushore, D. and T. Stark (2001), 'A real-time data set for macroeconomists: Does the data vintage matter?', *Journal of Econometrics*, **105**(1), 111–130.

to the extent that revisions themselves could be accurately forecast. If the revision of GDP to -2.7% in 2008:Q1 was partly forecastable at the time of the first release, policy could have responded much faster. To forecast what is happening to the economy, we may need to forecast the revisions process as well. Thus, the behavior of the statistics agency becomes a key ingredient when forecasting the actions of economic agents (firms, households, etc.) whose decisions determine the state of the economy.

But why would data revisions be predictable: surely a statistics agency will publish the 'best' estimates it can, which should rule out future revisions being predictable after the initial published estimate? Data revisions might be predictable if a statistics agency decides not to undertake any processing of its source data for fear of being accused of skullduggery, such as 'manipulating the statistics' for some political end. Suppose the agency receives a noisy estimate of the true state of the economy, which suggests the economy is doing better than expected based on information from other sources (possibly including a model of the economy). The chances are that this first estimate will over-state the correct value, but the agency decides not to alter the source data to improve its estimate, and so releases an estimate which is too high and will subsequently be revised down. If the agency did revise the initial estimate because it thought it was too high, and this revision was leaked, it might be accused of anti-government bias.

Inaccurate data do matter

To conduct monetary or fiscal policy effectively, a government needs reliable estimates of the current state of its economy. Such knowledge is available too late to help if policy-makers wait for the 'final' official statistics releases, which may be long after the window of opportunity to take effective action has shut, be it to cut tax rates to stimulate an economy at risk of slipping into recession, or to increase interest rates to take the steam out of an over-heating economy.

Not only do economists struggle to know where we are currently, but we face a further forecasting problem in that many of the measures that

are needed for forecasting the state of the economy are not directly observable. One of the key readings for policy is a measure of the degree of
slack in the economy, as typified by what is called the 'output gap'. It is
constructed by economists to measure how close to capacity the economy
is operating. The output gap measures the difference between the measured current level of activity in the economy and its 'potential' level of
output.

There are two problems a forecaster must now face. He or she needs
an estimate of the output gap 'in real-time', in other words, now, but can
only use an estimate based on data available *at the time*. Only unrevised
data—i.e., the first flash estimate or the latest estimate of output in the
previous quarter—are on offer and forecasters know that neither need be
a good estimate of the true state of the economy. Secondly, an estimate of
current potential output is needed, which is unobserved. Potential output
at a point in time is often calculated by smoothing over a few years of GDP
data both before and after that time. For historical analyses this might be
fine, but in real-time analyses, the future values relative to that time are
obviously not known. Obtaining reliable estimates of the output gap is
inherently difficult precisely because of the 'one-sided' nature of the data
available, coupled with the provisional nature of that available data. Real-
time estimates have to be made without recourse to the future data which
would provide a more accurate estimate of the underlying trend, possibly
by replacing the unknown actual values with forecasts.

In addition, 'output gaps' should relate the true level of activity to
its potential, rather than being based on uncertain estimates which will
subsequently be altered. For both of these reasons, real-time estimates
of 'output gaps' are likely to be markedly less accurate than historical
analyses would suggest. But it is real-time estimates that monetary or
fiscal authorities have to rely on to guide policy—little wonder policy can
sometimes seem to be misjudged in retrospect. We will return in Chapter
10 to consider 'forecasting where we are', often called *nowcasting*, to try
and improve provisional estimates of important variables.

Figure 3.1 illustrates another of the basic problems in measuring 'output gaps', namely what is 'potential output'? Here we are using linear
trends in the log of output per worker per year, the simplest possible model

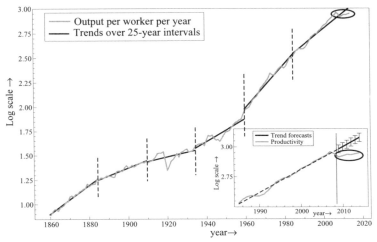

Figure 3.1: 'Output gaps' between realizations and trend rates of UK annual productivity growth (log scale).

of potential. However, a glance at the figure shows at least six major historical shifts in that trend rate of growth, with separate trends fitted to approximately 25-year periods marked by the vertical dashed lines, where the break in the trend was usually unanticipated. Inset in the graph is a smaller figure. This illustrates what a continuation of the pre-Great Recession trend would have led forecasters to anticipate from 2007 onwards (the bars around the trend forecast seek to represent a measure of its uncertainty, but are obviously wide of the mark). Is the huge gap a measure of the potential that could be regained by an appropriate economic policy? Or did the recession destroy capacity and the trend ended abruptly, so forecasts based on no trend would have been a much more accurate representation of the potential? Economic policy would be rather different between these scenarios. A decade of essentially no productivity increase is unprecedented over the past 150 years, the closest being the slow trend over 1895–1917. Are we in a new era of stagnation, or is productivity not being correctly measured with the burgeoning digital age? Forecasters have to resolve all of these issues, so forming a view of the likely future is not a straightforward activity.

> 'A trend is a trend is a trend, but the question is, will it bend?
> Will it alter its course through some unforeseen force, and
> come to a premature end?'
> Attributed to Sir Alec Cairncross, first Head of the UK Gov-
> ernment Economic Service.

Trends of various kinds will be a major focus of Chapter 6, where we also explain the inaccuracy of the uncertainty measure.

Chapter 4

How do we judge forecasts?

If Winter comes, can Spring be far behind?
Percy Bysshe Shelley, *Ode to the West Wind* (1, 57) in *Prometheus
Unbound, A Lyrical Drama in Four Acts, With Other Poems*,
London: Charles, 1820.

This chapter concerns what may surprise many readers, namely once a
forecast is not perfect, unlike Shelley's certainty (absent Ice Ages), it can
be difficult to judge how good, or bad, it is. This is because an imperfect
forecast can be wrong in any one of a number of ways. Some of these may
prove a minor inconvenience, but others might have catastrophic consequences depending on what it is that is being forecast, and why. In terms of
our motorist, it may not matter much (to either party) if she over-estimates
the journey time by 10 minutes and arrives 10 minutes early at her friend's
house. But under-estimating the amount of fuel required to safely return a
space rocket and crew to the earth after a lunar mission would constitute
an error of a different order of magnitude relative to over-estimating the
amount of fuel required.

If perfect forecasts were a reality, we would not need to consider the
costs of under- or over-estimating travel time or fuel required, because
such errors would not arise. Our motorist would arrive on time, and the

49

rocket would expend its last drop of fuel gently touching down on terra firma. In the real world, the various errors will have different costs (or losses), and, intuitively, a 'good' forecast will be one which induces behavior which makes the most catastrophic errors highly unlikely to occur. For example, the rocket will surely carry spare fuel, greatly in excess of the expected requirements of even the most cautious space engineer. *Ex post*, when the rocket touches down with spare fuel, this would be considered to have been a prudent forecast of fuel requirements rather than a reckless over-estimate.

Forecasts are made to inform decisions

Forecasts are made to guide actions. There is no inherent benefit to accurate forecasts, so they are usually made to improve the resulting decision making. The decision may be as simple as 'do I have time for a cup of tea before commencing my car journey?', or as important as 'how much fuel to take on the rocket?'. Consequently, forecasts should be judged based on how good the resulting decisions prove to be. Surprisingly, the forecast that is closest to the realized outcome may not be the best forecast. Anyone who has missed a train by 2 minutes will be well aware that arriving 10 minutes prior to the train's departure would have been a much better decision. Over-estimating travel time by 10 minutes, and arriving early, is less of a nuisance than under-estimating travel time by 2 minutes and missing the train.

The technical forecasting literature analyzes formal approaches to evaluating forecasts based on the decisions taken in response to them. In many ways, this is an idealized way of evaluating forecasts. Unfortunately there are large information requirements that limit its routine use in economics. We would need to know the losses associated with outcomes in different states of the world. Because of this demanding, and infeasible, requirement, we will only consider fairly standard forecast-evaluation methods. However, we will show how these can be adapted to capture the difference between the equivalent of arriving '2 minutes early' and '2 minutes late'.

Standard forecast evaluation criteria

Suppose our motorist made the same journey ten times in the last month, and in each case she recorded her actual journey time and her forecast of her journey time. How can we judge how good her forecasts were? One obvious consideration is whether she systematically under- or over-estimated her journey time. We could calculate the ten forecast errors, namely the actual journey time minus her forecast of how long the journey would take, and see whether the forecasts were consistently wrong in the same *direction*. Were all (or most) of the errors positive, suggesting that she systematically under-estimated journey time? Was she over-optimistic regarding how long the journeys would take? Were this the case, the forecasts would be said to be biased.

As well as the overall signs of the forecast errors, their magnitudes clearly matter for the accuracy of the set of forecasts. Large positive and negative forecast errors might cancel, so that the average of the forecast errors could be close to zero despite the forecasts being poor. Therefore the average error alone is deficient as a general measure of what it means for a set of forecasts to be good. The dispersion of the errors about their mean value (of zero for unbiased forecasts) determines the reliability, or precision, of the forecasts, and is usually measured by the sample variance. A large variance suggests that large forecast errors have occurred over the sample period, so may be likely to do so in the future. As we shall see later, obtaining good forecasts of the degree of precision of a set of forecasts is itself a key concern in some contexts. For now, we assume our interest is exclusively in judging the forecasts of journey time.

There is a large 'behavioral economics' literature suggesting that individuals tend to be both *over-optimistic* and *over-precise*.[1] In our context, over-optimism might be manifest in the motorist systematically under-estimating her journey times, and over-precision would arise if she under-estimated their variability.

---

[1] See Ulrike Malmendier and Timothy Taylor, (2015) 'On the verges of overconfidence', *Journal of Economic Perspectives* **29**, who also provide a short summary of over-confidence, which includes both over-optimism and over-precision.

The over-weening conceit which the greater part of men have
in their own abilities, is an ancient evil remarked by the philoso-
phers and moralists of all ages.
Adam Smith, *An Inquiry into the Nature and Causes of the
Wealth of Nations*, Book 1, Chapter X, W. Strahan & T. Cadell,
1776.

In these more enlightened times, we do at least allow that this 'conceit' is
not the exclusive preserve of men, as our motorist is taken to be female.

The mean squared forecast error (MSFE) is the most common method
of evaluating forecasts. It is the average (mean) of the squares of the forecast errors, and is equal to the square of the sample mean of the forecast
errors plus their sample variance. It takes into account the extent to which
the forecasts systematically lie on one side of the corresponding actuals,
as well as their lack of precision.

However, does a particular value of the MSFE indicate a good or poor
set of forecasts? There are at least two ways of answering this. The first
asks whether one set of forecasts is good relative to another set of forecasts. So this requires that we have a comparator or a benchmark set of
forecasts. The second is applicable if the forecasts are generated from a
formal model, in which case we can compare the MSFE to what might
have been expected based on how well the model had fit the data over the
past. For now we consider the first way.

In terms of our itinerant motorist, suppose she has a set of forecasts
given by AA Route Planner and a second set from Google Maps (GM).
The GM forecasts take into account local conditions, by making an adjustment for the busyness of the roads at the time the journey begins, and
this gives her reason to put more faith in these. But is she wise to do
so? After the event, we can calculate whether the MSFE of the GM forecasts is smaller than that of the AA forecasts across her ten journeys. One
MSFE will be equal to or smaller than the other, and this might well be
the GM forecasts. But of interest is whether that simply reflects sampling
variation or is a statistically significant difference in squared-error forecast
accuracy. In essence, had different journey-time outcomes been observed
due to chance changes in traffic conditions, would the ranking of the two

sets of forecasts by MSFE have remained the same? If not, the difference is probably due to chance, rather than superior forecasting.

The role of comparator forecasts in judging accuracy is just as relevant in the economics sphere. When looking at forecasts of macroeconomic variables, such as consumption, investment, and inflation, the forecast accuracy measured by the MSFE can vary widely, both across variables and across forecast horizons. It is not easy to see from MSFE values alone whether the forecasts are in any sense good. Does a large MSFE reflect the inherent difficulty in forecasting that variable, or are the forecasts of the variable poor? One approach is to use an alternative method of forecasting and see if the MSFEs from the alternative method are similar. So, for example, forecasts from surveys of professional forecasters could be compared to forecasts from simple statistical models. A large MSFE for both methods most likely reflects the greater difficulty of forecasting a given variable, whereas the survey forecasts for a variable would be deemed poor if they were clearly less accurate than those of a simple model based on limited information.

Everyone wins!

Unfortunately, rankings of forecasts based on MSFE-accuracy may also depend on what you consider. This is because the ranking may depend on whether we forecast the growth rate of a variable or its level, for example. Have a look at Figure 4.1(a). Which forecast would you say wins? Perhaps you would opt for forecast B, which, although it doesn't predict the trend, is usually closer to the actual data throughout the period. So, if forecast B wins, should we always use its forecasts? Possibly you might worry that forecast B will depart ever further from the trend in the future.

Now look at Figure 4.1(b). Rather than plotting the level of the data, we now observe the changes in the data. You could think of it as the growth rate of the data. If you had previously chosen forecast B as the 'best', have you now changed your mind? Forecast A seems to do a much better job of forecasting the growth rate, as B is almost always too low, which matches their tracking the trend, but not the level, and the level but not the trend.

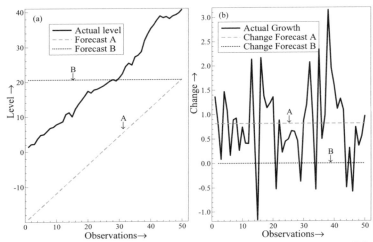

Figure 4.1: (a) Who wins: A or B?; (b) Now who wins: A or B?

Such a problem of deciding between A and B is well reflected in a famous quote:

> The Dodo suddenly called out 'The race is over!' and they all crowded round it panting, and asking 'But who has won?'
> This question the Dodo could not answer without a great deal of thought... At last the Dodo said *'Everybody has won, and all must have prizes.'*
> Lewis Carroll, *Alice's Adventures in Wonderland*, London: Macmillan and Co, 1865, p. 33.

Worse still, yet another model can be best on MSFE for forecasting, say, exports and imports, but a fourth model be best for forecasting the balance of trade, which is simply the difference between exports and imports. Despite the central role of forecast loss functions such as MSFE in evaluating forecast accuracy, the rankings of different models' forecasts are altered by whether we consider forecasts of levels, or changes, as in the illustration, or differentials. The choice between considering levels and changes might be casually taken, yet might have unexpected consequences.

Unequal costs of positive and negative forecast errors

In the introduction to this chapter, we argued that under-estimating and over-estimating the amount of fuel a rocket ought to carry would be associated with very different costs. Indeed, the consequences of under-estimating the required amount of fuel are so catastrophic that it is hard to imagine that a forecast which permitted this possibility (however remotely) would ever be countenanced. Even so, there are many instances where over- and under-estimates of similar magnitudes will not be viewed as equally undesirable, but, nevertheless, the worst of the two would not be regarded as at all catastrophic.

Consider our motorist. She may wish to guard against being late by aiming to arrive early. She may deliberately allow herself more time than she thinks is likely to be necessary when she embarks on a journey, so that for the majority of her journeys she arrives early. On the face of it, she systematically over-estimates her journey time, and her forecasts are biased. However, it can be rational for the motorist to make biased forecasts if the costs of arriving early and late (by the same amount of time) are different: the costs of arriving at the airport 5 minutes after the boarding gate closed are certainly not the same as the costs of arriving 5 minutes beforehand.

If she were to aim to arrive at the gate at the very last minute, whether or not she makes the flight would depend on events outside her control (heavier traffic than usual, slower progress through security and baggage-checking, etc.). If she left herself plenty of time she might still miss the plane, but this would be less likely, because more things would have to go wrong, or would have to go more badly wrong, to thwart her. In addition, the more uncertain she is about the expected journey time to the airport, the earlier she should plan to arrive to avoid being late. That is, her forecast of the variability of that journey time will play a role.

Once the costs of the forecast errors are allowed to depend on their signs, so negative and positive errors of the same magnitude are not equally costly, we move closer to the evaluation of forecasts in terms of their expected benefits across different states of nature. Suppose there are just two possible states—either it will freeze overnight (the Bad state) or temperatures will remain above freezing (the Good state) and there will be no ice on the roads. There are two actions the relevant authorities can take: they can grit and salt the roads (i.e., take action), or they can leave the roads untreated (and so do not act). As organizing and implementing gritting takes time if it is needed, the authorities have to decide in advance whether to act or not, and must do so on the basis of a forecast of the Bad state occurring. Since the Bad state either occurs or does not, the required forecast is the probability that the Bad state will occur. Say the weather forecast is for a 60% chance of freezing, so a 40% chance it will not: should the authority act? Obviously, the costs of the Bad state will be mitigated if the roads have been treated. But gritting the roads incurs a cost, and if the Good state occurs, then the authorities would not have wanted to do so.

The payoff when the roads are treated and the temperature falls below freezing is the value of the saving of life and the total monetary saving from avoided injuries and other damage from fewer accidents, less the cost of treating the roads. The payoff from not treating when it does not freeze is saving that last cost. Conversely, the cost of not treating when it freezes are additional deaths, injuries, and accidents; and the cost of treating when it fails to freeze is the unnecessary expenditure and messy roads.

In this relatively simple setting of two possible outcomes and two actions, when a numerical value can be assigned to each of the four payoffs, in principle the optimal action (either grit or do nothing) can be determined, *given the forecast*. The *expected* value of the forecast will depend on the actual probability of the Bad state occurring. As in other types of forecast evaluation, we need a number of forecasts of both states and their associated outcomes (whether the Bad state occurs or not) to make much headway in terms of determining 'how good' the forecasts are. We return to this issue when we discuss interval and density forecast evaluation.

In the economics sphere, the task is typically more complex. The monetary and fiscal authorities are faced by an unknown range of possible outcomes, with uncertain payoffs in those states which are difficult to measure, resulting from the many potential policy changes at their disposal.[2]

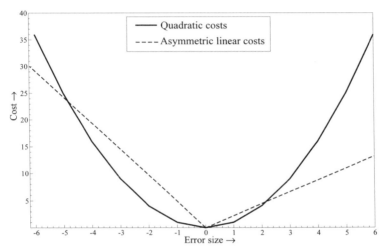

Figure 4.2: Asymmetric linear costs (thick dashed) and quadratic costs of forecast errors (solid).

There are a number of relatively simple cost, or loss, measures that can be used to evaluate forecasts without requiring a complete enumeration of all costs. Such loss measures typically capture some of the key elements described above. They can also allow for unequal costs, namely the extent to which over- and under-forecasts are weighted differently, called asymmetry.

The MSFE measure of forecast accuracy corresponds to a squared-error cost measure: the cost of any forecast error is measured by the

[2]See M. P. Clements, (2004) 'Evaluating the Bank of England density forecasts of inflation', *Economic Journal*, **114**, 855–877, for an exposition of 'decision-based' forecast evaluation, including a discussion of economic contexts.

square of that error. Negative and positive errors of the same magnitude are equally as bad, and their costs increase quadratically, so that an error of 2 has a cost of 4, but an error of 3 has a more than proportionate increase in cost of 9, and so on. Common asymmetric cost measures might have costs increasing linearly on either side of the origin of a perfect forecast but at different rates, or costs might increase linearly on one side of the origin, but increase much faster on the other. Figure 4.2 shows how these two measures differ, where negative errors are worse than positive when evaluated by the asymmetric linear cost function shown.

However, once we allow for losses being asymmetric, the 'best' forecast, in the sense of minimizing the expected loss, will necessarily also depend on the forecast of the uncertainty. Why this is an essential ingredient follows from the discussion above of the motorist: the greater the uncertainty, the more the motorist needs to aim to arrive early to avoid the costly outcome of missing the flight. Of course the optimal forecast will also depend on the extent of the asymmetry. The greater the costs of under-forecasting, the higher will be the optimal forecast relative to the forecast that would minimize expected squared-error loss, and hence the greater the magnitude by which the forecaster will aim to over-forecast on average. This implication matches our conclusion above on ensuring more than enough rocket fuel. When loss is symmetric, these concerns do not apply: the optimal forecast does not depend on the degree of forecast uncertainty.

Economic forecasters may also have asymmetric loss measures, so that apparently systematic forecast errors do not necessarily imply that the forecaster is guilty of poor forecasts. Government forecasters may seek to reduce the pressure for public-sector wage increases by publishing inflation forecasts that are overly low, for example, but even private-sector forecasters may not have maximizing accuracy as their one and only objective. Forecasters' own objectives may depend on a variety of factors that may not be well aligned with producing the most accurate forecast possible.

Chapter 5

How uncertain are our forecasts?

If you can look into the seeds of time
And say which grain will grow and which will not,
Speak then to me.
William Shakespeare, *Macbeth* (I, iii)

Chapter 2 showed that forecasts will almost never be perfect: there are many factors affecting any forecast that are not foreseen or cannot be taken into account in advance. In terms of a forecasting model, all effects that are not included when making the forecast are subsumed into the error term. As a first approximation, we suggested that the error term might be assumed to be Normal. That assumption allowed us to estimate how far the forecast is likely to be from the realized value, and we gave some examples in terms of the standard deviation of the error term. However, that standard deviation, or its squared value the variance, has to be estimated from the available data. Moreover, absent evidence to the contrary, it is then assumed to be the same in the future. But this need not be the case, contributing to the forecast uncertainty itself being uncertain.

Modeling and forecasting uncertainty

A forecast of that uncertainty seeks to correctly measure the variance of the forecast distribution in question. If this is large, then outcomes a long way from the mean of the distribution are more likely than if the variance were small. Our motorist is more likely to suffer the costs of being late had she not taken appropriate action, namely had she not realized that her actual journey time might be quite different from her forecast journey time.

The simplest way of forecasting the variance is using an historical variance estimator, as we have done above. For our motorist, that would be the variance of the errors she has previously made in forecasting her journey time. Or, perhaps rather better, she might use just the variance of the more recent of those forecast errors, if, as seems likely, the more recent past is a better guide to the future than the more distant past. For example, errors made in the distant past, when there was less traffic on the roads, may under-estimate the likely magnitude of future errors. Conversely, other changes might point in the opposite direction: for example, mechanical failures and the ensuing delays may be less likely nowadays. The key point is that, when the distributions of forecast errors shift over time, for whatever reason, using less representative observations from the distant past may be undesirable.

The important message is that we also have to forecast the extent of the uncertainty around our forecast making that uncertainty uncertain. If the outcomes we are trying to forecast come from a relatively well-behaved process, say with a constant mean and variance, our forecasts of uncertainty can be fairly accurate. In such a setting, there are three main sources contributing to the estimated uncertainty which we discuss in turn.

Most forecasts based on replicable procedures are made from models. Such models involve equations that connect data on several variables. The first source derives from mismeasurement of those variables, discussed in Chapter 3. The next two concern how the variables are connected, and what is not included in the model. So far we have avoided giving algebraic formulations of models, although at this stage some simple formalism will help the exposition. Few readers will not have heard of our opening equation.

Perhaps the most famous equation ever is Albert Einstein's $E = Mc^2$ which relates the energy, E, contained in matter to its mass, M, multiplied by the speed of light, c, squared. Knowing the mass and the speed of light, the energy can be predicted.

Who could have imagined three such disparate entities being so tightly connected, ushering in the nuclear age!

That equation has three 'variables', E, M and c, which are linked by several components called 'parameters'.

The link of E to M is precisely unity: doubling the mass doubles the available energy.

The link of E to c is also unity, but c has an additional parameter of ^{2} to denote squaring.

Einstein's theory of relativity makes c constant in a vacuum, so we cannot double it: c^2 is the fixed proportion linking E and M.

Here, all the parameters are known precisely, and the relationship is *exact*. Thus, E on the left-hand side of the relationship is precisely equal to Mc^2 on the right-hand side. All the determinants of E have been accounted for, so there is no *error*.

At a much less exalted level, our motorist's forecasts depend on her 'model'. Her model is based on her map, which depicts the distances that need to be traveled on roads of different types, for example, major roads, city streets, and country lanes with legal speed limits in miles per hour. The parameters of her model are the average speeds she might expect to achieve on these different types of road. Multiplying the distances to be traveled on each type of road by the inverse of the likely average speeds, and adding these up, provides a forecast of travel time. But, unlike Einstein's equation, her forecasting equation does not hold exactly: there is an error term which captures everything that affects the variable being forecast other than what is explicitly included in the model. Here omitted effects include delays from congestion, accidents, unexpected bad weather, and road works. It may be too difficult to quantify such effects, so they are not included in her forecasting model, but left to be part of the error. Doing so increases the magnitudes and the variability of her errors, and hence the uncertainty around her forecasts.

The boxed material on the next two pages describe a simple economic model that could be used for forecasting, the parameters in such a model, and the sources of uncertainty from estimating those parameters and the error terms of the model.

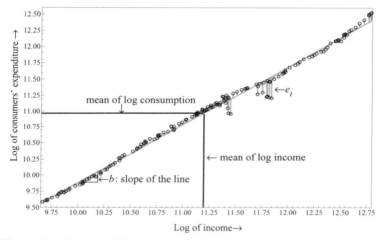

Figure 5.1: Relationship between the log of aggregate consumers' expenditure and log of aggregate income in the UK.

To illustrate, we use the celebrated 'Keynesian consumption function' of British economist John Maynard Keynes, one of the most influential economists of all time. His equation concerns how consumers' expenditure responds to changes in income. Figure 5.1 illustrates the relation between consumers' expenditure and income (both in logarithms) using data for the UK, showing the data points and deviations e_t from the line of 'best fit'. The mean of log consumption is 10.97 and that of log income is 11.2 as shown, and the slope of the line is denoted b.

Like $E = Mc^2$, formal forecasting models have parameters linking their variables.

Consider the simple economic model $y_t = a + bx_t + e_t$.

A variable called y_t, measuring consumers' expenditure at time t, is explained as a plus b times another variable x_t namely income.

The subscript t (for time) shows that the model will be related to time-series data.

The equation has an error e_t, assumed to have a mean of zero and be Normally distributed.

e_t is the difference between actual consumption spending y_t, and the level of $a + bx_t$ predicted by the equation given income x_t.

The parameter a is called the intercept, and the slope b reflects the impact of a change in x on y.

However, the magnitudes of the parameters in economic models, and many others, are rarely known. This leads to the second source of uncertainty that will affect forecasts: estimating the numerical values of any unknown parameters in the model.

Econometrics has invented many ways to estimate the values of unknown parameters in a model. The most common is 'Ordinary Least Squares' (OLS). This estimates a and b by choosing their values to minimize the sum of the squared vertical distances between the actual values y_t and the resulting fitted values. As those deviations vary with changes in the values given to a and b, we choose the estimates to minimize the sum of the squared errors.

The deviations e_t from the line in Figure 5.1 are those whose sum of squares is minimized to estimate the slope b, which here is 0.9 leading to estimating a as 0.85.

As b increases, the line becomes steeper, whereas increasing a shifts up the point at which the line crosses the vertical axis.

Although Figure 5.1 relates $\log y_t$ to $\log x_t$, the principle is the same.

The variability in estimating the parameters a and b depends on the values taken by the x_t and the e_t. A wide spread of the former helps pin down the value of b and hence of a, whereas noisy errors—i.e., with a large variance—makes that harder, and also adds to the uncertainty of future outcomes.

As the sample of observations changes, different numerical values will be obtained for these parameters, and that variation creates uncertainty.

Remarkably, by assuming the model is correct, we can derive reliable measures of both sources of variability, despite having just a single sample of data from which to do so. From that data, we can establish the statistical significance of the estimates, and test whether the unknown true value of the gradient, b, is different from zero, thereby checking there is actually a relationship between the variables.

The third source of forecast uncertainty derives from the variance of the errors, usually assumed to stay the same for the future errors. However, the errors e_t also include other non-modeled factors which affect y_t besides x_t. Were any of those factors systematic, and able to be modeled, they would typically be included in the model as additional explanatory variables.

The equation in the box above (p. 63) would have a constant marginal propensity to consume out of income given by b, and a declining average propensity to consume, given by y/x, so, the savings rate would rise as income increased when $a \neq 0$.

Fortunately, in the absence of measurement errors, the two variances determining forecast uncertainty can be added to give the overall estimated forecast error variance. Although standard deviations are more convenient for many purposes, they cannot be added, so we use variances here. Both of these sources, based on assuming a constant model up to and after the forecast origin, were included in our earlier calculations of fan charts. Usually the estimation uncertainties around unknown parameters are taken to follow Normal distributions, such as that shown in Figure 1.2, albeit with different variances depending on how 'well determined' the parameter values are. We have taken the errors to be Normally distributed, so the combined uncertainty is calculated as the variance of a Normal distribution. How well does that work?

Introducing time allows 'dynamic' or 'lagged' relationships to be formulated such as $y_t = a + bx_{t-1} + dy_{t-1} + e_t$, where the current level of spending y_t is influenced by x_{t-1} and the value y_{t-1} in the previous period.

Spending habits could explain such connections, so today's expenditure depends on how much was spent last period.

Models with lagged variables naturally lend themselves to forecasting by forging a temporal link between a variable at t and variables at $t - 1$, or earlier.

If the explanatory variables are known at the forecast origin, denoted T, they can be used to provide a forecast of the left-hand-side variable at time $T + 1$: $\widehat{y}_{T+1} = a + bx_T + dy_T$, where the 'hat' reminds us it is a forecast.

Figure 5.2 plots some data that we have generated by a dynamic model to have a mean of 20 and a standard deviation of 1 by taking the Normal distribution in Figure 1.2, centering it at 20, then drawing numbers at random from that distribution to obtain the sequence recorded as the solid line. Figure 5.2 also records bands showing the forecast uncertainty for a simple model. In Chapter 1, we expressed the standard deviation as a percentage of the average, which would be 5% here. An important feature of a standard deviation is that its units are the same as the average: if the mean is in feet, hours, or $millions, the standard deviation is also in feet, hours or $millions. The fitted model explains 75% of the data variation, and the estimated standard deviation is close to 1.

In Figure 5.2 we are forecasting 1-step ahead, then updating the data variables to the actual outcomes before forecasting the next step ahead, and so on for the 8 forecasts. Most of the forecast uncertainty comes from the variability of the unpredictable future errors. All the forecasts lie within

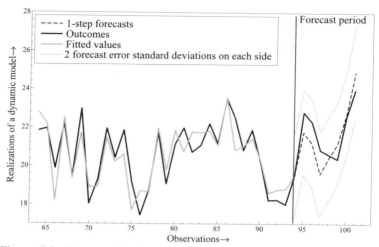

Figure 5.2: Two standard error forecast uncertainty bands (dotted lines) around the 1-step ahead forecasts (thick dashed) with the later realizations shown (solid).

the 95% bands, so here not only are the forecasts accurate, those bands correctly represent the uncertainty.

Since we know how the data were generated, we can fit the correct model then forecast from it, so we expect that the calculations will be accurate both for the point forecasts and their spread. Thus, when all the assumptions are correct, both the forecasts and their uncertainty are as accurate as expected.

Unfortunately, reality is rarely so kind. The forecasts shown in Chapter 2 were for increasing forecast horizons, so 1-step ahead, then 2-steps, and so on till the end period of 1989:Q2. As each successive forecast is going further into the future, the uncertainty increases, whereas for the 1-step forecasts in Figure 5.2, the estimated uncertainty stays relatively constant. The fan charts in Figures 2.6 and 2.7 also used two forecast standard errors. As those Chapter 2 figures showed, the band of uncertainty increased the further ahead the forecast, as more events can happen that were unknown at the forecast origin. Indeed, Figure 2.6 also showed that the resulting measure of uncertainty can be seriously wrong if a location shift occurs, as all the outcomes lay well outside the anticipated interval. When the magnitudes of forecast errors are widely at odds with what we expected, then this calls into question the reliability of our model. Figure 2.7 showed that, on this occasion, the problem was due to a legislative change and could be rectified soon after its occurrence.

In practice, the variance of the error term might not be constant over time. In some settings, it may change in a way that is nevertheless fore-castable. If so, then the uncertainty bands, and the assessment of the quality of the forecasting model, would need to take this variation into account. Forecasting the uncertainty about the central forecast is also nec-essary when using an asymmetric cost measure, as discussed in Chapter 4. The greater the expected uncertainty concerning the outcome—i.e., the less precise the forecast—the more a forecaster will deliberately bias the forecast in the direction of the greater cost, to reduce the likelihood of making a costly error.

In terms of our motorist, we argued that she would need to estimate how *uncertain* her journey time is likely to be whenever the costs of ar-riving late significantly exceed those of being early (such as arriving at an airport to catch a flight). Then the more uncertain that she perceives her journey time to be, the longer she should allow for her journey.

Interval forecasts

Sometimes the perceived uncertainty about the future is formalized into an interval forecast. The thin dotted lines in Figure 5.2 also provide an interval forecast. A point forecast is (usually) a measure of the central tendency of a forecast distribution, such as the most likely outcome (the mode), or the expected value (the mean). The point forecast carries no information on *how* likely the forecast is thought to be, or on the degree of uncertainty surrounding the forecast. It might be the mean of a uniform distribution (i.e., the midpoint of a range of values, all of which are held to be as likely to occur as every other value, as with casting dice), or the mode of a highly concentrated symmetric distribution such as the Normal, where values greater than, say, a tenth of a percentage point from the mode are highly improbable. An interval forecast gives a range in which the outcome will occur with a certain probability, and so would immediately tell us which of the above two cases applied. Sometimes the interval forecast is an adjunct to a point forecast, but it can also be the object of interest in its own right. We recommend thinking about forecast-error bands such as those in Figure 5.2 as describing interval forecasts, which reminds us that the entire interval is a forecast even when the forecast standard error is constant over the forecast horizon.

Above we have illustrated the estimated uncertainty around forecasts by fans, error bars, and bands. The choice depends on the desired clarity of communication and the purpose of the forecasts. Fans allow a finer grading of the estimated uncertainty by the lightness of the colors further from the center. Bands are less intrusive than bars, but need distinctively different lines to that of the forecast itself. However, all representations reflect the same underlying numerical calculations of estimated uncertainty.

A 95% interval forecast is a statement that the interval will contain the actual value 95% of the time (i.e., with probability 0.95). The actual value either will or will not fall within the interval. Therefore, to evaluate how good the interval forecasts are, we need a sequence of interval forecasts with their associated outcomes having the same probability of being correct. The 'coverage rate' is the probability that the outcome will fall in the interval. Intuitively, if this is 95%, we would expect the percentage of our sample of interval forecasts which contain their actual outcomes to be close to 95%. In Figure 5.2, the 95% interval forecasts actually contain the outcome 100% of the time, but that is close enough, given there only 10 forecasts. We can formally test whether differences between the observed coverage rate and the expected coverage rate are statistically significant— could such discrepancies have arisen by chance or, alternatively, are they sufficiently large to indicate the intervals have a coverage rate larger or smaller than 95%? Perhaps less intuitively, we would expect the 'hits' (when the interval correctly contains the outcome) and the 'misses' (when the interval does not contain the outcome) to arise independently anywhere in the sample when the errors are independent. If a hit is observed in one period, the probability of observing a hit next period remains 95%, just as a head on one toss of a coin does not affect the 50-50 chance of a head on the next. This assumption would fail if there were patterns in the hits and misses, so that misses were clustered together. Such might occur if the forecast-error variance varied over time, perhaps in a systematic fashion, but the forecast of that variance was constant. Then the interval forecasts would not be wide enough in turbulent periods, compared to relatively tranquil times, to ensure a constant 95% probability of the interval containing the outcome at each point in time. There would most likely be too many misses in the volatile periods.

'Density' forecasts

In our discussions, we have generally supposed there is a distribution for journey times and forecasts thereof, and have usually taken both to be Normal distributions as in Figure 1.2. However, their means and variances may change over time, even though our motorist is assumed to be undertaking the 'same journey' each time, in the sense that she is always driving from her house to the same friend's house. Although the journey is made once a week on a Saturday afternoon, say, she starts at different times. Hence her actual and forecast journey times may change for a host of reasons (e.g., her friend lives in Finsbury Park, and Arsenal are playing at home at the Emirates Stadium that Saturday, or it is a 5.30pm, instead of a 3pm, kickoff, and so on). Rather than reporting her journey time as Normally distributed with her estimated mean and variance, the realized times could be summarized in a histogram as in Table 5.1. Against each journey time in 10 minute intervals we record the probability that she assigns to her journey time being within that interval (this might be based on her past experience of journey times). For example, she believes there is a 10% chance that her journey time will be between 35 and 45 minutes, a 20% chance it will take between 45 and 55 minutes, a 40% chance between 55 and 65 minutes, a 20% chance between 65 and 75 minutes, and a 10% chance of being as long as between 75 and 85 minutes.

Table 5.1: Imaginary histogram for our motorist's journey time

Journey time (in minutes)	Probability (%)	Cumulative probability (%)
35–45	10	10
45–55	20	30
55–65	40	70
65–75	20	90
75–85	10	100

Notice that the probabilities sum to 100%, shown as the 'cumulative probability' in the third column. The first and last bins are 'closed', so no probability is assigned for the journey taking less than 35 minutes, or more than 85 minutes, even though we know such events could occur. However, a histogram provides an incomplete picture relative to knowing that the forecast density is Normal (or is some other known distribution). For example, the histogram bin probabilities are symmetric, but the histogram does not show that the mean, mode and median are all 60 minutes. Nor can one tell that the probability assigned to 60 is greater than that assigned to 58 or 62, or is indeed less.

To ascertain that level of detail, the records would need more, and hence shorter width, bins, although one could imagine that even assigning meaningful probabilities to just five bins could be challenging. Let us suppose for the moment that our motorist has in mind this kind of histogram for her journey time on each occasion she sets off, albeit that may seem far-fetched. Nevertheless, in principle the task is well posed, and is easily understood, so our motorist will not be released from such considerations just yet. In practice, creating a histogram may be less unrealistic than we might think. The average human motorist might not (almost certainly does not!) regularly undertake such a task, but we suspect that soon such information could be routinely provided in computer-driven cars, or by the next generation of sat-navs. For example, such devices already estimate journey time, and it would be relatively simple from that to calculate a standard deviation for the forecast errors over the last few (similar) journeys, and hence to provide an estimate of the forecast density. Figure 1.3 showed a forecast density around an expected journey time, albeit non-Normal as there seems to be a greater probability of events that lengthen journey times unexpectedly than events shortening a journey more than anticipated.

Evaluating 'density' forecasts

The forecast distributions of interest to many economists come in the form of survey respondents attaching probabilities that key variables will fall in pre-set bins as in Table 5.1. Suppose we have a probability assessment, using a Normal density, or just a histogram, with estimated values for the mean and variance. The key question is, how accurate is that probability assessment compared to the corresponding distribution of outcomes? Given a single forecast and the actual journey time, it is not possible to infer much about the quality of the probability assessment. If the histogram was that given in Table 5.1, and the actual journey time was 90 minutes, then we might be less inclined to praise the motorist's forecasting abilities compared to if the journey took an hour. But it is difficult to assess how good any type of forecast is—a point forecast, interval forecast, or a density forecast—with such little information.

Suppose our motorist has kept a record of both her actual journey times and forecasts for her last few journeys, collected in a histogram. Now the situation does allow an evaluation of how good her forecasts are. Suppose, for example, the outcomes almost always fall in the left half of the forecast distribution. When we use the histograms to calculate the probabilities of observing shorter journey times than were actually recorded, these probabilities are predominantly less than one half. Such calculations would be accurate if we knew the forecast density, but some interpolation is required with a histogram because of its coarser record.

Suppose the outcome for the histogram in Table 5.1 is 65 minutes. As 65 is the upper limit of the third bin, the sum of the probabilities assigned to the first three bins is $10\% + 20\% + 40\% = 70\%$. However, if the outcome happened to be 58 minutes, we would have to interpolate the probabilities within the bins. One way of doing so is to assume that the probability within the 55–65 bin is uniformly distributed, so we could calculate that $[(58 - 55)/(65 - 55)] \times 40 = 12$ of the third bin mass is less than 58, so the outcome would be $10\% + 20\% + 12\% = 42\%$.

The situation just described suggests the histogram is allocating too much probability to longer journey times which do not materialize. We would expect journey times to fall in the left side of the distribution around half of the time. Similarly, we would expect a quarter of the probability mass to be to the left of the lower quartile (the smallest 25% of journey times). In other words, if we calculate the probabilities of observing lower values than the outcomes, we would expect to find probabilities of less than one quarter approximately a quarter of the time. Across all the pairs of her forecasts and their outcomes, we would roughly expect a given percentage of the outcomes (25% or 50% etc.) to lie to the left of that percentage.

The requirement that probabilities of observing values smaller than the actuals of one half should occur roughly half of the time and those of one quarter roughly a quarter of the time are instances of an approach to density forecast evaluation known as the probability integral transform. The probability integral for a given density is the probability of observing a value smaller than the actual. When the forecast density is the correct density for the data, then the probability integral transform would be uniformly distributed between 0 and 1. Consequently, the probability it is less than one quarter is one quarter, and the probability it is less than one half is one half, and so on, matching the cases we just enumerated.

In terms of economic forecasting, we consider the aggregate histogram forecasts of the quarterly US Survey of Professional Forecasters (SPF).[1]

---

[1] See   https://www.philadelphiafed.org/research-and-data/real-time-center/survey-of-professional-forecasters/.

The individual survey respondents provide probability distributions for inflation and output growth in the form of histograms. We average these over individuals for each survey. Each survey provides histograms for the annual percentage real GDP growth rate between the current year, and the previous year, and for the annual inflation rate, defined in the same way. For surveys which take place in the first quarters of each year, the forecast horizon is effectively one year ahead, as there is relatively little information available on the current year, whereas for the fourth-quarters of the year surveys the forecast horizon is effectively one quarter.

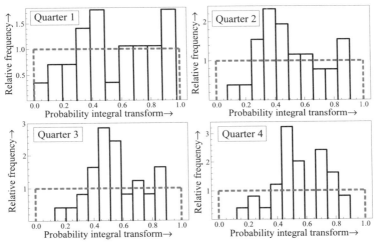

Figure 5.3: Histograms evaluating the survey outcomes for real GDP across four quarters.

Forecasters are assumed to target an early-vintage release of the outcomes as discussed in Chapter 3. That is, probability integral transforms are calculated by comparing the histograms to the advance or first estimates of calendar-year output growth and inflation released towards the end of January of the year following the year being forecast. Using data from the quarterly 'Real Time Data Set for Macroeconomists' maintained by the Federal Reserve Bank of Philadelphia, Figures 5.3 and 5.4 present histograms of the probability integral transform values for the SPF aggregate histograms for real GDP growth and inflation, respectively.[2]

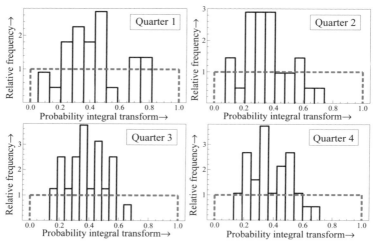

Figure 5.4: Histograms evaluating the survey outcomes for inflation across four quarters.

We present the values for each survey quarter separately. The top-left panel relates to the first quarter of the year surveys, so it reports results for year-ahead forecasts, the top-right panel shows results for second-quarter surveys, and so on. For an accurate set of density forecasts, the values shown should resemble realizations from a uniform distribution, so the histograms should be flat: the dashed boxes at unity show what such a uniform distribution would be in each panel. For GDP, there are too few

---

[2]There is a data set for each quarter that contains only those data that would have been available at a given reference date: subsequent revisions, base-year and other definitional changes that occurred after the reference date are omitted. As discussed above, probability assessments in the form of histograms provide an incomplete picture, so we approximate the histograms by the 'best fitting' Normal distributions and base the calculations on those.

low probability values. This suggests that the aggregate SPF probability assessments tended to be too pessimistic, at all horizons. The histograms tended to assign too much weight to low rates of growth. The plots for inflation in Figure 5.4 were also overly pessimistic in that too much probability was placed on high-inflation outcomes which failed to materialize. This is apparent from the relatively low number of high probabilities, especially at the shorter horizons.

Chapter 6

Are some real world events unpredictable?

> Some things are so unexpected that no one is prepared for them.
> Leo C. Rosten, *Rome wasn't burned in a day: the mischief of language*, Garden City, N.Y.: Doubleday, 1972. Taken from http://www1.secam.ex.ac.uk/famous-forecasting-quotes.dhtml

Why were events such as the 2008 financial crisis, the Brexit referendum, and the Trump election apparently so unpredictable? There are a number of possible explanations.

First, there is the sheer complexity of the phenomena we wish to forecast. As an example, consider population growth. The key determinants are naturally birth rates and death rates, but these in turn vary with health, nutrition, sanitation, medical innovations, longevity, and so on, which in turn depend on a huge number of influences, including economic development, government policy, wars, etc. It might seem that the forecaster's task is hopeless. However, these factors might be expected to change by only relatively small amounts from period to period, so that provided the forecast horizon is relatively short it might still be possible to generate reasonably accurate forecasts, or, at least, forecasts with the expected degree of accuracy (calculated from the past performance of the model in use). Moreover, we noted in Chapter 2 that a model need not capture all the relevant influences to achieve its expected degree of forecast accuracy. Perhaps surprisingly, a model that is poor in terms of its 'correctness' need not lead to bad forecasts. For example, the Ptolemaic system is far from a realistic model of planetary motions, but nonetheless it predicted lunar eclipses reasonably well for several thousand years. A motorist's map likewise may always have been incorrect, so forecasts for all trip times are somewhat wrong, but no worse than expected. Thus, the complexity of the world by itself need not preclude useful forecasts.

Second, serious events that culminate in sudden and large effects can be ushered in by minor surprises or small changes in a system. In terms of our motoring analogy, serious traffic delays can occur, even without an extreme event as a cause. For example, when a moderate volume of traffic passes through a roadworks that reduces the number of lanes, no problems may arise. If the traffic volume increases only a little, horrendous congestion can result. Such effects are classified as 'non-linearities' and 'regime switches'. Up to a point, increasing the traffic density has only a modest effect on travel time; but beyond that point, increased traffic density leads to serious delays, with gridlock as an extreme outcome. Similar situations arise in economics. Once we know about them, non-linearities can be modeled, but still may catch out the unwitting economic forecaster. For example, within a certain range, an exchange rate might respond roughly proportionally to a balance-of-payments deficit; but the exchange rate might suddenly nose-dive as concerns over bank, or even government, solvency develop. As another example, business cycle booms and busts in the economy may reflect an inherently non-linear, regime-switching process, with ceilings of full capacity and floors where governments or central banks intervene to stabilize the situation.

Third, consider a world that changes so fast that, by the time a map has been compiled, it is immediately out of date. Some roads marked on the map no longer exist, perhaps from major landslides or earthquakes, or may be unusable from a bridge collapsing, and the map fails to show the new ones that have opened. Route planning would become exceptionally hazardous, and large forecast errors would abound, depending on whether the destination required traveling on a now non-existent road. Estimating the forecast errors' variance would itself be hazardous, as the forecast errors would depend on which roads had vanished and which replacements could be used as substitutes. No simple corrections for the resulting mis-specifications could be calculated: sometimes forecasts would be accurate, and sometimes very poor. Fortunately, we do not live in a world that changes quite so drastically all the time—but there are features of this sorry tale that do occur.

For example, a totally unexpected event that must have caused catastrophic forecast failure in the journey times of the many travelers involved was when a pedestrian bridge on the UK's M20 motorway was hit by a truck and collapsed on one of the busiest travel days of the year, although fortunately no-one was injured. This is a real-world case of a location shift in the journey times that day.[1] Sudden road closures from bad accidents, or (especially in the UK) long delays at rail stations and airports from a snow storm—even when forecast!—all lead to location shifts in those days' journey times.

We contend that the economic equivalent of this third explanation, namely like a collapsed bridge, is primarily responsible for forecast failure, when a model's forecasts are far less accurate than expected (as in Figure 2.6, for example), with observed values in the extremes of forecast-error distributions. Of course, such events may well interact with model mis-specifications and non-linearities to exacerbate the forecast failure, but, without the location shift, they would not have induced failure.

In some periods, our third explanation is an apt analogy for the situation an economic forecaster can find him- or herself in. For this and other reasons, some forecasting agencies maintain several models: the Bank of England's approach to modeling and forecasting includes using a suite of models rather than a single model. Very different forecasts from their models then warn that some of the models must be at odds with reality: later outcomes may help to isolate the source of that problem. We now consider 'economic earthquakes' in more detail.

---

[1] See http://www.bbc.co.uk/news/uk-england-kent-37204050.

Sudden unanticipated shifts: When the ground moves

Economic forecasts go badly wrong because of unexpected events which shift the distributions of economic variables. As an example, we consider UK per capita GDP. Figure 6.1 records the historical data on the annual percentage growth in UK per capita GDP from 1874 to 2016.

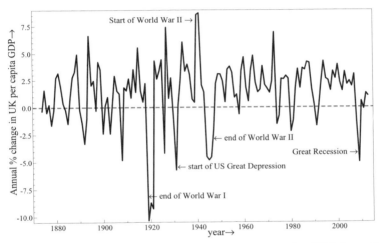

Figure 6.1: Annual percentage growth in UK per capita GDP from 1874 to 2016.

The horizontal axis records the time, and the vertical axis shows the percentage change. This time series is erratic, and has varied between -10% in the crash at the end of World War I, and $+8\%$ at the start of World War II. Many 'extreme events' have occurred as well as the World Wars, especially the huge recessions after such wars ended, including the Great Depression and the recent Great Recession among others: there are plenty of economic potholes.

The shifts in the growth rate in Figure 6.1 are so large that we cannot assume the series of values constitute random draws from a Normal distribution with a *constant* mean (or variance) across the historical period. If the mean was constant over time, the use of the historical average would provide a reasonable forecast. That is, we forecast that the growth rate of the economy in the future will be equal to the historical average growth rate up to that point. This is called an unconditional forecast, in the sense we are not making use of a model that conditions the forecast on the value of the series at the forecast origin: use is not being made of the state of the economy at the time the forecast is calculated.

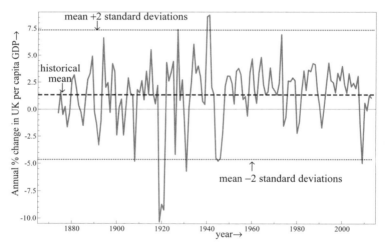

Figure 6.2: ± 2 standard deviations around mean annual percentage growth in UK per capita GDP.

Over the last 250 years, per capita GDP growth in many developed countries has risen from near zero to about 2% per annum, with standard deviations around their mean growth rates of about 3% pa. Say the forecast is set to 2% per annum, then a forecast interval which would include the outturn most of the time (i.e., around 95 times in 100) would have to be

2% ±6%. Thus, all one could say is that next year's annual GDP growth will be between a fall of 4% and a rise of 8%! Such a forecast is neither useful nor very informative.

Figure 6.2 illustrates this situation for the time series of annual percentage growth in UK per capita GDP from 1874 to 2016 shown in Figure 6.1. The historical mean growth rate was in fact 1.35% pa, shown by the long-dashed line, with a standard deviation of 3%. The dotted lines show 1.35% ±6%, and, as can be seen, there are very few occasions when observations fall outside such wide bands. The bands need to be so wide because of the 'extreme events' that have occurred as discussed above. Nevertheless, as forecast-error standard deviations they are too wide to be useful.

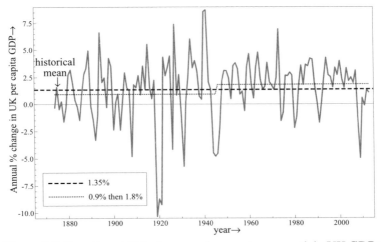

Figure 6.3: Location shift in the annual percentage growth in UK GDP per capita at 1945.

In fact, although it is hard to spot from Figure 6.1, average annual per capita GDP growth in the UK has *not* been constant across the whole period. The dotted line with the kink in 1945 shown in Figure 6.3 records the separate mean historical growth rates pre and post that date, and reveals a *doubling* from 0.9% pa to 1.8% pa, a fundamental location shift for living standards.

At 0.9% pa, it takes about 80 years for real incomes to double, whereas at 1.8% pa, they double every 40 years.

To simplify calculations by using 4 epochs of 40 years, over the 160 years between 1856 and 2016, living standards would have risen 4-fold had the former rate continued throughout, as against 16-fold if the UK had always grown at 1.8% pa, and the nearly 8-fold that was achieved in practice.

In our forecasting context, the dotted line is systematically closer to most of the post World War II outcomes so forecasts based on the sub-sample mean would have been better most of the time (albeit, worse on the few occasions when GDP fell). A keen eye might notice that the volatility of the time series also changed after 1945 when Keynesian economic policies were adopted (we call this ocular econometrics), with the standard deviation falling from 3.6% to 2.1%. Consequently, using the mean of the somewhat more recent past of the data would reduce the expected uncertainty to 1.8% ±4.2%, a range from −2.4% to 6%, working well most of the time but missing the fall of 5% in 2009, and leading to forecast failure had that mean been used as the forecast.

Shifts in the mean values of variables over time are referred to by economists as *non-stationarities*: more generally, the term applies when distributions of events change over time.[2] A stationary series is one where those features are constant, and hence the time series is really ahistorical, in the sense that actual dates do not matter much. Of course there may be intermittent ups and downs of business cycles, so the dates of peaks and troughs matter, but any long section of data will 'look like' any other with the same mean and variance. However, non-stationarity is clearly a

---

[2]A recent non-technical explanation is provided by Hendry and Felix Pretis, *All Change! The Implications of Non-stationarity for Empirical Modelling, Forecasting and Policy*, Oxford Martin School Policy Paper, 2016.

characteristic of economies: technology, legislation, politics, and society all change over time, markedly affecting living standards, the variability of unemployment, the level of inflation, and so on.

Modern econometrics has devoted considerable effort to developing models of non-stationarity, and their models fall into two distinct classes. The first includes models of regular and persistent changes (called 'stochastic trends' because there are apparently random fluctuations around the average growth). Interest in such processes date back more than a century.[3] The second class includes models of 'structural breaks', which are large sudden, and usually unanticipated, shifts.

Flocks of 'black swans'

> All swans are white; this is a swan; therefore it is white.

This Aristotelian syllogism was believed in Western Europe for centuries, untill its inhabitants learned in the 18th century that swans were black in some southern-hemisphere countries, such as Australia. Despite that knowledge, in English, a 'black swan' still refers to an unlikely, or even impossible, event.[4]

In Chapter 1, we assumed that the random error component generating the outcome (or, more precisely, the realized value relative to the forecast value) was a 'known unknown', in the sense that it is a random draw from a fixed Normal distribution, with a known mean and variance (perhaps determined from past data). In that setting, we are able to make precise probability statements about the magnitude of the error: for example, the probability that the error will be between -2 and $+2$ forecast error standard deviations is 95%. Even if we were to allow the variance to change over time, in essence the analysis is unchanged. We would simply replace the in-sample estimate by the forecast value, which will typically depend

---

[3]Hendry and Mary Morgan, *The Foundations of Econometric Analysis*, Cambridge University Press, 1995.

[4]See Nassim Taleb, *The Black Swan*, Random House, 2007, for 'the black swan theory' describing rare and possibly unpredictable events.

on information available at the forecast origin. We still might happen to get a 'large' realization of the random error, but this would be 'unlikely', and could be thought of as a 'black swan'.

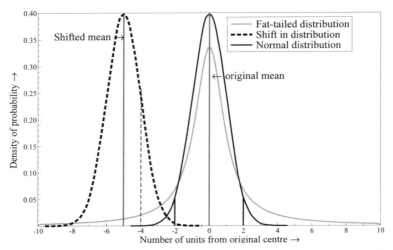

Figure 6.4: Sometimes see a 'flock of black swans' when location shifts make the new ordinary seem unusual relative to the past.

Returning to the example of rolling two dice, we know the probabilities when they are perfect cubes with a different number on each of the six faces. However, there is an unknown probability distribution when the dice are loaded. To envisage a shifting distribution, consider a magnet being switched on and off to alter the outcomes from those loaded dice, depending on which individual rolled them. Betting on the basis of 'fair' dice will lead to systematically mis-forecasting the outcome. An occasional cheat will lead to an unlikely outcome, say 4 sixes in a row for the person controlling the magnet and none otherwise. However, if the perpetrators of the fraud were too greedy, always penalizing the other participants, so getting say 12 sixes in a row, we could call this a flock of black swans. Once too many very unlikely outcomes are seen, trouble may ensue.

Similarly, the first black swan ever seen may have been unpredictable to a European, but surely the 5th cannot still be regarded as 'highly unlikely'? We have already seen the solution in Figure 2.2: a shift in the mean of a distribution makes the earlier outcomes look discrepant relative to the new mean. 'Flocks of black swans' therefore seem to appear after sudden, unanticipated large changes, or location shifts, in the distributions which were previously generating the outcomes. So forecasts are now systematically wrong, and the errors we make are not bounded by the randomness in the 'known unknowns'. Figure 6.4 illustrates where outcomes to the left of the vertical dashed line have a greater than 80% chance of happening after the shift, but are highly unlikely from the original distribution. In the next chapter, we consider forecasting in a black-swan world, but first we consider that other main source of non-stationarity which we call stochastic trends.

Trends and their ilk

There are two main classes of trend: stochastic, which vary around an increasing or decreasing trajectory; and deterministic, which change at a uniform rate in a given direction. Like any other feature of a journey or an economy, the growth rates of either can change, but for the moment we leave that complication aside.

Figure 6.5 records an artificial-data example of a stochastic trend growing on average at 2.5% per period, with 1- through 8-step ahead forecasts. The fitted model in Panel (a) is the stochastic trend which generated the observations, whereas Panel (b) reports the same data with the best fitting deterministic trend and its forecasts. The widths of the interval forecasts are -2 to $+2$ forecast-error standard deviations.

Clearly the Panel (a) model fits the data much more closely, and, although it initially has a much smaller interval forecast, by 8-steps ahead the two panels exhibit similar uncertainty. Importantly, the width of the interval forecast from the deterministic trend remains the same, and would

still be 11 units 100 observations later! Conversely, the stochastic trend
interval forecast is growing rapidly and would span a huge range of uncertainty 100 observations later. This is because the impacts of the errors
cumulatively affect the stochastic trend, but are *assumed* to only influence
the deterministic trend for the one observation when they hit. Here that
assumption is incorrect, so the future uncertainty is poorly estimated.

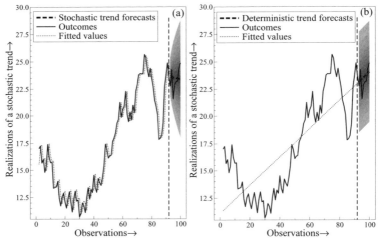

Figure 6.5: Stochastic trend data. Panel (a): stochastic trend model with its
interval forecasts; Panel (b): the same data characterized by a deterministic
trend model.

Now consider the converse: the data are generated by a deterministic
trend growing at the same rate of 2.5% per period with random Normally
distributed errors added. Again we forecast from both models. Figure
6.6 shows the outcome. Although the data generated by stochastic and
deterministic trends look very different, the patterns of the interval forecasts look similar: Panel (a) grows rapidly, whereas Panel (b) stays the
same width, but correctly in this second case provided the trend does not
'bend'.

Moreover, appearances to the contrary notwithstanding, the deterministic trend model in Panel (b) of Figure 6.6 actually fits the data far better than the stochastic trend (residual standard deviations of 1.15 versus 1.60 for the stochastic trend), as it should do because it generated the data. That is not obvious from a glance at Panel (a). Warning: the eye and mind are very bad at perceiving *vertical* discrepancies between two lines such as the fitted and actual values in Panels (a) of both Figures 6.5 and 6.6. In order not to be fooled, notice that the fitted values in Panels (a) lag behind the corresponding outcomes, so they are often up when the data go down and vice versa, leading to many large vertical gaps, most noticeable in Figure 6.5 around observations 80–90, and near the forecast origin and again around the observation numbered 60 in Figure 6.6.

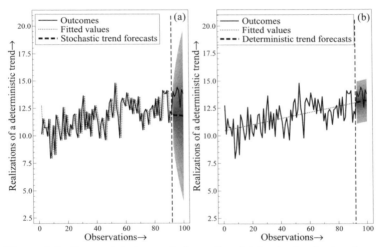

Figure 6.6: Deterministic trend data. Panel (a): stochastic trend model with its interval forecasts; Panel (b): the same data characterized by a deterministic trend model.

Why does the type of trend matter?

Three issues follow: first, can we tell which case is the correct one in real-world data? Second, what can we do to tackle trends? Third, in the immortal phrase for forecasters, 'the trend is your friend–till it doth bend'.

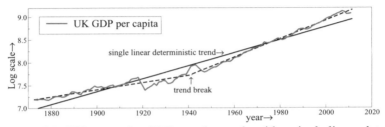

Figure 6.7: UK per capita GDP on a log scale with a single linear deterministic trend for the whole period, and two sub-period linear deterministic trends split at 1945.

We have already seen the third above with a shift in the mean growth rate of UK per capita GDP, which is of course, a shift in the trend, as Figure 6.7 for the level of UK GDP shows. A split trend around World War II is a far better description of the data than a single linear deterministic trend for the whole period.

Next, we have actually already handled trends by calculating growth rates, or changes, and plotted those in Figure 6.1 above. Because changes remove the non-stationarity from the stochastic trend, such processes are also called difference stationary (i.e., the changes are stationary although the levels are not), but that assumes no location shifts occur. Similarly, because the deterministic trend model is assumed to have stationary errors, it is called 'trend stationary', which is something of an oxymoron.

We now comment on the first issue: can we tell which trend formulation is appropriate? In essence, we want to compare the data that would result from a stochastic trend to what would be obtained if the economy was instead driven by deterministic trends—but we can only run it once for any given time period. A close equivalent is to fit a more general model

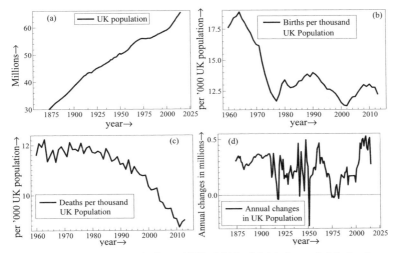

Figure 6.8: (a) UK population, 1875–2015; (b) births and (c) deaths per thousand, 1960–2012; and (d) changes in the population over 1875–2015.

that includes both types of trend and see which does better—is either irrelevant? If so, the other is more likely to have generated the observed data. Unfortunately, economic data are subject to many influences and shifts, so discrimination can be difficult, but both kinds of trend could be allowed for when empirically modeling.

Figure 6.8 provides an example of population data, shown for the UK, exhibiting both characteristics of stochastic trends and location shifts. The size of a country's population varies with changes in birth rates, net migration, and death rates, so is influenced in turn by a huge number of influences leading to increasing longevity and lower infant mortality. It is also affected by social decisions concerning marriage ages and rates, interacting with the numbers of females in the fertility age range and their desired family sizes, location choices, and social behavior concerning life style choices such as smoking, drug taking, and diet. Key discoveries such as vaccination, antibiotics, carbolic for cleaning, anesthetics, and birth control can cause persistent shifts in the means and variances of the data on both births and deaths.

Figure 6.8 Panel (a) shows a strong but varying upward trend, with some falls, typical of a stochastic trend. Panel (b) reports the large impact on UK birth rates of the introduction of oral contraception in the mid-1960s, and the persistently lower levels since then—a marked location shift. Panel (c) records the large declines in death rates since 1960, with fluctuations around the downward trend. The low of less than 9 deaths per thousand does not entail that most people in the UK must be living to over 100: the population has been increasing from net inward migration of almost 200,000 per annum, many of whom are young. Finally, Panel (d) shows the overall effect on the annual changes in population, which is somewhat erratic, but not trending. There is a fall from World War I and the flu' pandemic that followed it, but the largest fall is from net outward migration after World War II. Forecasting such changes is difficult, especially several years ahead.

Trends can cancel

Stochastic trends can wander widely, even when they are growing on average. Figure 6.5 showed a large drop at the start of the period and again after observation 80. Thus, it is unsurprising that forecasts from such models will have wide interval forecasts that increase as the horizon grows. But all is not lost: both forms of trends can cancel when modeling several variables. Although there are few good motoring analogies for what we call 'trend cancelation', consider two scenarios. In the first, our motorist and a friend set off at the same time from the same place with the same destination, but choose different routes, so are buffeted by different delays that cumulate (like stochastic trends) so arrive at widely separated times. Naturally, their trends do not cancel. In the second scenario, our motorist is towing her friend to a garage, so the two are never separated and are only buffeted by a single set of common delays. Imagine that each vehicle is viewed as having a separate journey, where the delays are in common so cancel between them: the distance the cars are apart stays the same with a rigid tow bar.

A similar phenomenon occurs in economics, though obviously not because of such rigid links. Both disposable income and consumers' expenditure have trended greatly over the centuries, increasing 7–10 fold since the start of the Industrial Revolution, yet the savings ratio (their difference relative to income) has stayed within fairly narrow bounds, rarely going outside the range zero to 20% (or 40% in countries such as Japan and China as they grew rapidly). Thus, the stochastic trends in income and expenditure must be in common and cancel when calculating savings. This is called cointegration, where stochastic trends are common and cancel in combinations of variables. Consequently, there are two ways to tame stochastic trends: work with changes, or find cointegrating combinations. In his Nobel Prize Lecture awarded for the discovery of cointegration, Sir Clive Granger threw a string of beads on the lectern and noted that they stayed connected, whereas a handful of beads would have scattered in all directions.

Location shifts can also cancel

It may not surprise that there are also two ways to handle location-shift non-stationarity. The first is by 'co-breaking' combinations, where two location shifts cancel, just like two common trends. Figure 6.9 Panel (a) illustrates one location shift and (b) shows a second at the same time but of a different magnitude. The dotted lines show what the forecast failure would have been if the location shifts were ignored. Subtracting twice the second shift from the first results in complete cancelation, as shown in (c), removing the forecast failure for the first variable. While precise and complete cancelation is unlikely as in the example here, shifts at nearby dates may cancel most of an impact.

However, to cancel a location shift takes two variables, and the shift can only be removed for one combination, so the other variable will still be badly forecast. That takes us to the second way, which is even closer to the solution we noted for stochastic trends, namely to calculate the change

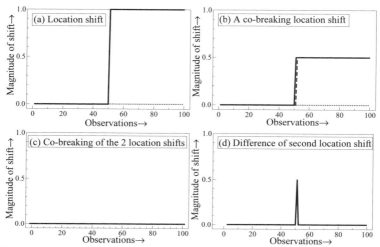

Figure 6.9: (a) A location shift from 0 to 1 at time 50; (b) a second similar-timed but smaller location shift; (c) the first shift minus twice the second canceling the shift; (d) the effect of differencing the second location shift.

in the second variable, thereby differencing its shift. Doing so results in an impulse, corresponding to the spike shown in Figure 6.9 Panel (d). Now there is one bad forecast, at the time of the shift, then the error reverts to zero. The effect is shown in Panel (b) by the dashed vertical line, confirming that the location shift is correctly tracked when the forecasts in differences for the second variable are cumulated to provide the forecasts of the level.

There are even motoring analogies for tackling location shifts, which we have seen earlier can greatly affect both the journey times and the resulting forecast errors. First, co-breaking takes some imagination, but a possible setting is where a bridge across a river was suspected of being so fragile that plans were in place for an alternative route. Thus, when that bridge was closed, or even collapsed, the army corps immediately installed a Bailey bridge that opened at once, canceling the forecast error that would otherwise result. In a rather bad pun, the two changes co-break. Differencing would correspond to finding an alternative route that took roughly the same time. We will consider these 'solutions' in more detail shortly.

Chapter 7

Why do systematic forecast failures occur?

> Because of the things we don't know we don't know, the future is largely unpredictable.
> Maxine Singer, (1997) 'Thoughts of a nonmillennarian', *Bulletin of the American Academy of Arts and Sciences*, 51, 2, p. 39.

Our intrepid driver has witnessed red traffic lights, congestion, road works, and a collapsed bridge forcing a diversion. She has already had to stop in a lay-by to phone her friends and warn them that her initially predicted journey time is no longer accurate, and she will be arriving much later than her forecast. The journey time initially forecast already suffers from forecast failure, as there will be a significant deviation of the forecast from the outturn. Had she made this journey repeatedly facing all of these hazards on each journey, yet maintained the same forecast journey time, not only would she be a very unlucky driver, but she would have made systematic forecast errors. Once she becomes aware there is a collapsed bridge and consequently a diversion from her usual route, yet she fails to account for that information in forecasting future journey times, her forecasts will continually suggest an expected journey time that is less than the actual outcome.

In Chapter 6 we discussed the non-stationarities that characterize the economic system, in terms of shifts in distributions and structural breaks. In this chapter, we explore how the nature of the economic system causes persistent forecast failure when we use certain types of forecasting models. We explore examples of forecast failure in economics, analogous to those our poor driver has experienced. We will also consider some examples where relatively accurate forecasts could have been made despite huge changes in the economy. In so doing, we will explain the reasons why systematic forecast failures occur. The 'bars', bands, or fans around the forecasts earlier in this book show ±2 standard errors, which correspond to a 95% probability that the outcome will lie within this interval, under the assumption of a constant Normal distribution. This implies that we would expect 5 out of 100 outcomes to lie outside those standard error bars on average. An outcome that lies well outside that range suggests forecast failure, and a sequence of outcomes that lie outside such standard error bars is termed systematic forecast failure.

Some impressive forecast failures

Examples of forecast failure in economics abound, but let's first consider Figure 7.1 which records year-on-year percentage changes in Japanese exports plotted monthly up to 2008. Exports are fairly volatile, with swings of up to ±20% per annum. We built a model of Japanese exports to forecast future export growth, which produced the forecasts shown from 2008 to 2015, perhaps to be used for guiding an industrial strategy. Both the central tendency (dashed) and the interval forecasts (dotted lines) are shown for a 95% probability that the outturns will lie between the bands.

In mid-2008 Japanese exports fell by 70% relative to the previous year, partly due to the weakness of the global economy and the appreciation of the Yen against the Dollar. The magnitude of the decline was huge, and quite unlike any realizations prior to 2008, so would be difficult to model *ex ante*. Figure 7.2 shows the dramatic swings in net exports, with both

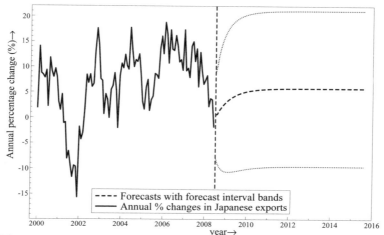

Figure 7.1: Annual percentage changes in Japanese exports with forecasts and the forecast interval bands.

the sudden fall and the subsequent rebound. Note the change in scale on the vertical axis—a 20% change looked large initially, but is dominated by the big crash in the forecast period. Recall that the data are measured as the annual change in exports, so the rebound in mid-2009 is in comparison to the fall in mid-2008.

The third author was visiting the Bank of Japan in mid March 2009 to teach a short forecasting course when the first data on the dramatic drop in exports was received (then 'just' a 40% fall). The reaction was a rather horrified surprise, and the immediate question arose as to what April's export numbers might look like—to which Hendry replied it would be more of the same: but as the graph shows, it was even worse.

Clearly, trying to forecast up to 7 years ahead is in general a tall order. But in this case, as Figure 7.2 reveals, the forecasts 7-years out are more accurate than the disastrous short-term forecasts. In a sense, this is really the result of export growth rates returning to more normal levels, varying

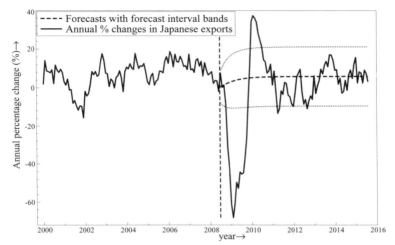

Figure 7.2: Annual % change in Japanese exports: forecasts and outcomes.

over a similar range to those before the crash, than any genuine knowledge of the Japanese economic environment 5 to 7 years into the future.

What about forecasting just one month ahead? This ought to be an easier task, to the extent that the factors and trends that determine next month's outcome would already be in motion to some extent. Moreover, short-term planning is essential for businesses. Toyota needs to have an idea of exports in the next month to organize production levels and control stockpiling. Figure 7.3 records the 1-step ahead forecasts, which are the 1-month ahead forecasts for the annual change in exports, thereby using data up to 1 month prior to the forecast month for each forecast.

Exports declined dramatically from September 2008, but the forecasts from the model used here were far too optimistic for each month until February 2009. The outturns lie well outside the forecast intervals. So trying to predict the annual change in exports just 4 weeks out is proving to be much more difficult than we might expect. The forecasts are then reasonably accurate again through mid-2009, but miss the rebound in export

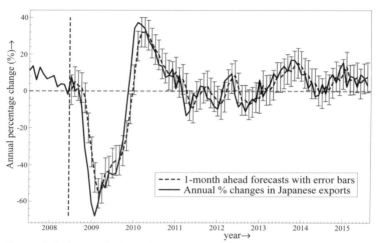

Figure 7.3: 1-month ahead forecasts and outcomes for Japanese exports.

growth, and become far too pessimistic: the outturns are systematically above the 1-month ahead forecasts throughout late 2009. Once the annual growth in exports returns to historical levels, the forecasts are then back on track, with no evidence of forecast failure over the 60 months from September 2010 on.

An informative way to view these forecasting mistakes is to look at the squared forecast errors, given in Figure 7.4. The forecast errors are just the actual change in exports minus the 1-month ahead forecast of that change. This forecast error is squared so positive errors (where the forecasts are lower than the outturns) and negative errors (forecasts are too high) are compared equally. The squared errors are plotted with the forecast period on the horizontal axis, where the shaded boxes highlight the months of forecast failure. These shaded areas correspond to the big swings in export growth, yet the same model performs well after mid-2010.

Once again, we are left with the uneasy suspicion that it is more the behavior of export growth which determines the accuracy of the forecasts,

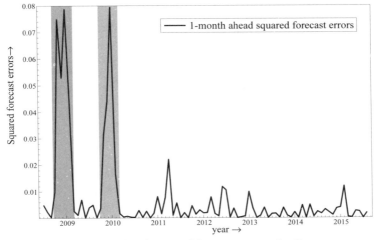

Figure 7.4: 1-month ahead squared forecast errors for Japanese exports.

and that the nature of the model and its forecasts *per se* are of secondary importance. When exports dive, the forecasts are too high. When exports rebound, the forecasts are too low. Given the nature of the forecasts generated by typical economic models, this can be a useful way of thinking about what is happening. The model is forecasting export growth of a 'normal rate'. When actual export growth happens to be close to this normal rate of growth, the forecasts are reasonably accurate, but otherwise not. This all seems a bit topsy-turvy: we want forecasts which accurately point to where the economy will be, rather than waiting for the economy to move into the model's cross hairs to claim a success. Below we consider why a broad class of economic models inadvertently give rise to this feature.

Missing systematically

Let us look at another example. It is well documented that economists failed to forecast the Great Recession following the financial crisis. As Prakash Loungani notes, the consensus forecasts of economists had not predicted that a single economy would fall into recession, even by September 2008, a full year after the bank run on Northern Rock, a British Bank, originally a Building Society, that then failed in September 2007.[1]

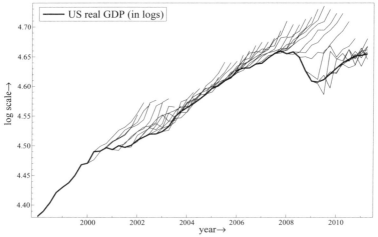

Figure 7.5: A 'hedgehog' graph of 8-quarter ahead forecasts of US GDP.

However, could there have been problems in forecasting GDP even before the financial crisis? Take a look at Figure 7.5, which plots the log of US real GDP at a quarterly frequency from 1998, with forecasts commencing in 2000:Q1. For each quarter, there is a sequence of 1-step to

---

[1]See Ahir and Loungani (2014): http://voxeu.org/article/predicting-economic-turning-points. Also see Loungani, (2001), 'How accurate are private sector forecasts? Cross-country evidence from consensus forecasts of output growth', *International Journal of Forecasting* **17**, who wrote 'The record of failure to predict recessions is virtually unblemished'.

8-step ahead forecasts plotted.[2] So in 2000:Q1, our model produces a forecast for 2000:Q2 (denoted the 1-step ahead forecast) all the way through to 2002:Q1, i.e., a 2-year ahead forecast for GDP (so is an 8-step ahead forecast for quarterly data). Then, one quarter later in 2000:Q2, we have additional information upon which a further sequence of 1-step through 8-step ahead forecasts are made. Each of these sequences of forecasts is plotted in Figure 7.5, along with the outturns over this period.[3]

What do you observe? The recession starting in 2008 is clearly evident *ex post*, with positive growth being forecast even as the economy nose-dived. Only when the recession was almost at its trough, in 2008:Q4, do the forecasts foresee negative growth. But there is something a little more subtle in the Figure. Almost all of the forecasts lie above the outcomes for the entire decade. There was not just forecast failure over the recession period, but this Figure shows systematic mis-forecasting over much of the forecast period. Does the graph make you think of a hedgehog, with it's spines all spiking upwards? We call graphs like these hedgehog graphs as the forecast errors have the same sign systematically for long periods. This is clear evidence of systematic forecast failure, which arises here because the trend rate of growth slowed down at the start of the new century, but the model continued to extrapolate the higher growth rate of earlier years. Although some adjustment of forecasts closer to outcomes is visible over 2003–2006 as the growth rate increased, the problem recurs with another slowdown after 2006.

Examples of 'hedgehog' forecast graphs abound. Figure 7.6 records productivity, measured by output per worker per hour, rebased to equal 100 in 2009:Q1.[4] The solid line plots the actual productivity over the following 8 years, with the forecast trajectories starting from a variety

---

[2]The data are real GDP, billions of chained 2009 dollars, quarterly, seasonally adjusted annual rate downloaded from the St Louis Fed.

[3] The 'forecasts' are obtained by us from an equation where the current outcome is explained by previous values, after impulse-indicator saturation, commencing with 8 lags, and selecting at 1% using *Autometrics*, both discussed in Chapter 9, but without re-selection for each recursive forecast.

[4]Based on a graph in the *Financial Times*, October 5, 2017, by Chris Giles, showing Office of Budget Responsibility (OBR) projections. Also see Tim Harford, *Financial Times*, May 30, 2014: http://www.ft.com/cms/s/2/14e323ee-e602-11e3-aeef-00144feabdc0.html.

of dates all showing systematically higher predictions of productivity than the outturns. Both Figures 7.5 and 7.6 demonstrate that systematic forecast failure occurs empirically, as there are prolonged periods in which forecast errors have the same sign.

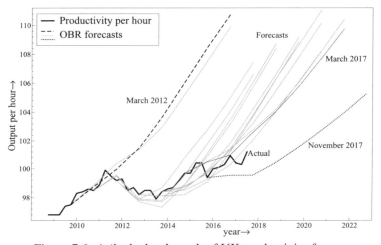

Figure 7.6: A 'hedgehog' graph of UK productivity forecasts.

There are two different reasons why a 'hedgehog' outcome might occur. First, the model is really just extrapolating the past into the future, so, when the growth rate slows, the forecasts lie above the later outcomes: the recession merely highlights that effect. Second, the type of model widely used in economics keeps converging back to the previous trend (which is the location in terms of changes), irrespective of what the data do—until the model is revised. If the data fall well below the previous in-built mean of the model, the forecast will be for a *rise*, as that is what is necessary to regain that mean. Thus the forecast is in the wrong direction, a notable feature of Figure 7.5 as the Great Recession is entered. This second issue will recur later.

We don't always fail!

The previous two examples may have left you feeling pessimistic about the ability of economists and their models to forecast, but there are numerous examples of successful forecasting within economics. Forecast failure is latched on with glee by the media, delighting in the chance to expose our glaring errors. But we rarely hear about the success stories: these are not deemed newsworthy.

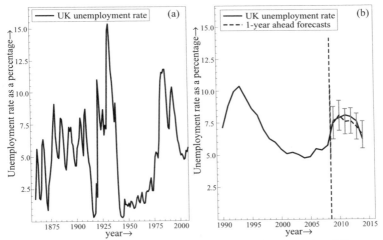

Figure 7.7: UK unemployment, annual data with 1-year ahead forecasts.

Take a look at Figure 7.7. On Panel (a) is a plot of the UK unemployment rate, extending back to 1860, measured annually. This is a difficult series to predict. There have been huge and sudden changes in the unemployment rate, with very different regimes evident over the 150-year period. Take, for example, the response of unemployment to the end of World War I, when unemployment went from near zero as everyone was employed in the war effort to 11% in just a year or two. Contrast this with the response after World War II, where, due to very different economic policies such as the Beveridge Reforms and the Marshall Plan, as well as a more Keynesian-style approach, unemployment remained well below 2% in the years following the end of the war. However, a large rise in unemployment occurred with the 1970's oil crises.

So how well do we fare in forecasting unemployment over the Great Recession? Panel (b) shows the unemployment rate plotted from 1990 onwards, with 1-year ahead forecasts given from 2009 onwards. The forecasts are derived from a model where the unemployment rate rises when the real interest rate exceeds the real growth rate, and falls otherwise. Along with the forecasts, their ± 2 standard-error bars are plotted, within which the actual unemployment rate should lie 95% of the time. The forecasts are remarkably accurate for a period that experienced substantial structural change, with the outturns lying almost directly on top of the forecasts. Spectacular forecasting success for an economic model: there is no forecast failure for such an unemployment model over this 'Great Recession' period given its explanatory variables.[5]

Looking at past episodes of large swings in unemployment, very large changes in real GDP have tended to feed through to unemployment with a strong effect fairly quickly. Had a similar relationship held over the Great Recession period, it would have resulted in a much larger increase in unemployment this time round than occurred. A combination of factors, such as quantitative easing, more flexible labor markets, more part-time work and shorter contract hours, an increase in underemployment, people moving out of the labor force during the recession, more self-employment, and more flexible pay enabling firms to weather weaker demand without lay-offs, probably all helped limit the rise in unemployment. The forecasting model used above did not model any of these interactions, and yet it forecasts well, so the plethora of effects appear to have approximately canceled out.

We have seen that some forecasts fail and some succeed. So what distinguishes the two? We next explore that very issue, helping us to explain the successes and failures just seen.

---

[5]For further details, see Castle, Clements, and Hendry, (2016), 'An overview of forecasting facing breaks', *Journal of Business Cycle Research* **12**.

What changes matter most for forecast failure?

We've seen some good forecasts and some very poor ones: so what is going on? Forecasts can be made in many ways, but the ones we are considering are model-based. Models have three basic components: deterministic terms including means and trends; stochastic variables such as GDP and inflation; and unobserved terms that we have bundled into the error. For the moment, just consider cases without trends: let's assume these have been handled by cointegration or differencing. A non-trending stochastic variable can always be written as the sum of its mean value and the deviation from that mean. Imagine doing so, then we can add the means of all the explanatory variables in the model to give an overall mean around which variation occurs. That mean is the equilibrium of the model.

As an example, reconsider $y_t = a + bx_t + e_t$. When c is the mean of x_t, we can rewrite that equation as $y_t = (a + bc) + b(x_t - c) + e_t$, so $(a + bc)$ is the overall mean, or equilibrium.

An equilibrium is a state from which there is no inherent tendency to change, just like a ball sitting at the bottom of cup. Gently shaking the cup moves the ball around, but it keeps reverting back to the bottom. We cannot imagine either road journeys or economies in which there are no shocks, but, if small shocks do not persist, journey times would be near their mean value and an economy would settle towards its equilibrium. Most economic models fall into a broad class which aims to capture both a well-defined equilibrium and a dynamic process by which its economy adjusts to that equilibrium. Such models can be very sophisticated, with non-linear adjustments leading to varying speeds at which the economy is expected to return to equilibrium. But the principle of adjustment to equilibrium is pervasive in economics and economic models almost always have such equilibria embedded within them.

When a model is fitted to past data, it's equilibrium will match that of the actual data over the historical period. Because we are not able to observe shocks, models assume future errors will on average be zero, which is their expected mean. The resulting forecasts should only differ from the outcome values by the effects of the unforecastable shocks. Consequently, as we look further ahead, the model's forecasts will approach its equilibrium. So, provided the model's equilibrium does match the equilibrium of the (non-trending version) of the economic system generating the data, then the future data will fall in the model's cross hairs.

The changes that really matter for forecast failure boil down to what is happening to the model's equilibrium relative to the actual data. Suppose the equilibrium of an economy shifts. Then a model that is not immediately amended to reflect that change will generate forecasts based on adjustment to the wrong equilibrium, so will deliver inaccurate forecasts: if that state continues, systematic forecast failure is the inevitable result.

In the previous box, the equilibrium is $(a + bc)$, so that could change if the intercept a shifted, or the parameter b changed, or c, the mean of x, altered, or many combinations of these.

Then the mean of y would shift from $(a + bc)$ to $(a + bc)^*$, say.

Figure 2.1 illustrated such a shift for journey times.

As a concrete example, suppose that our car driver plans to save 10% of her income each period, on average (that is, in equilibrium). Last period she was faced with some unexpected outgoings, such as the need for a new set of tires (all those additional miles traveled in detours!), and her savings were much less than the 10% she had planned. Suppose a forecaster knows that her equilibrium savings ratio is 10%, and hence that she plans to rein in her spending to save more this year. Assume the forecaster is also able to forecast her income for this coming year. Armed with this knowledge, it ought to be possible to provide a forecast of her expenditure that is reasonably close to her actual expenditure. Of course the forecast will not capture any unexpected items that might cause her spending to depart from the planned levels: these are captured by the random error term in the model of her behavior, and have an expected or mean value of zero. She may well 'over-spend' again, of course, as a result of unplanned but necessary incidental expenses. However, the resulting inaccuracies in the forecasts of her spending are likely to be fleeting relative to those resulting from unforeseen changes in her equilibrium savings ratio. For example, suppose her perception of the economic outlook worsens and she plans to save 20% of her income from now on, unbeknown to the forecaster. The forecaster will now systematically over-predict her spending. Almost all the examples of forecast failure that we observe are due to shifts in long-run means that are not modeled. Shifts in long-run means tend to be noticed *only well after the event*. With large ones, we can just eyeball the data: but Figure 6.7 shows a key shift that took decades to be discovered. Nevertheless, we should be able to incorporate many past shifts in our forecasting models to improve how well they capture the data variation. A decade on from the financial crisis, *ex post* modeling of it is much more straightforward. Hindsight is a wonderful thing! Foresight is harder.

Learning from past mistakes

We have considered the possibility that the equilibria towards which the forecasting model and economic system adjust may diverge over the forecast period due to shifts in the latter. However, this makes the somewhat heroic assumption that the two match during the sample. But, as we have seen, change is constantly occurring in the economy. Figure 7.8 shows UK annual wage growth and price inflation over the last 150 years with the solid line recording large shocks and mean wage inflation over 10 different epochs.[6] There have been periods in which inflation is near zero or negative, and periods in which inflation has been well above 15% per annum, with peaks of 25% and troughs of -22%.

If we wished to forecast future inflation based on this historical data how would we go about it? There are a number of options. One is to throw up our hands in despair of ever being able to model the complexity of the historical record of inflation and simply to look at the recent history, in the hope that this will be a reasonable guide to future inflation movements. Or we might attempt to model the whole period, but allow the parameters on the explanatory variables to vary over time. There are various approaches

---

[6]The latter are often called outliers, defined as changes that lie outside a given number of standard deviations from the mean, such as $\pm 2s$.

for doing so, including allowing the parameters of a model to 'drift' in a manner that can be modeled; or supposing that there are a small number of distinct 'regimes' (e.g., high or low inflation), and that the data we observe at any point in time are generated from shifts between these regimes; or to try to capture the shifts in a general way. Before considering possible solutions, we need to explore the role of shifts in more detail.

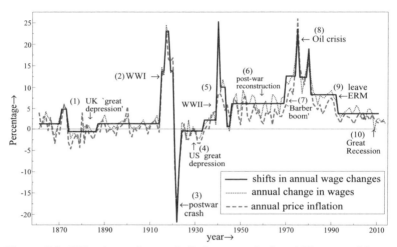

Figure 7.8: UK price and wage inflation over the last 150 years with step shifts.

A shift in an equilibrium is a key case of a location shift, and Figure 7.8 shows some large shifts, from a near zero average in the 19th Century, almost hitting 25% during World War I, with a huge drop immediately after, remaining mainly negative in the inter-war period, then again very high during World War II, 5% through the post-war reconstruction, rising towards 15% again around the Oil Crises, then steps down to about 2.5% after leaving the Exchange-Rate Mechanism (ERM) in October 1992. Within each epoch, the 'local equilibrium' is a fair representation of the data, so, although there are deviations therefrom, knowing only that equilibrium would have allowed passably accurate forecasts. However, many of the equilibrium shifts were abrupt, and would not have been foreseen much in advance, if at all. Forecasting 1915 inflation in 1914 would have been sadly awry, as would the post-World War I crash, when prices and wages fell by more than 20%, whereas forecasting most inflation rates from 1890 to 1913 by the 1890 value would not have been greatly amiss.

The model in the two boxes above (pp. 105, 106) just related y_t to x_t contemporaneously, so to forecast y_{T+1} from time T one would already need to know x_{T+1}. To avoid that problem, most forecasting models use past values, so would relate y_t to x_{t-1}, say.

A common forecasting approach just relates y_t to its own past value y_{t-1}, sometimes assuming the link is unity, so forecasts y_{T+1} by y_T, as in $\widehat{y}_{T+1} = y_T$. This is called a random-walk model.

It has no equilibrium to shift, an issue of importance in Chapter 8.

What do forecast failures entail?

By now we have a good understanding of what contributes to systematic forecast failure. But what does such failure entail for the models used for forecasting? Surprisingly, forecast failures need not entail that the underlying theory is invalid or even that the forecasting model is flawed. Apollo 13 was a space craft launched in April 1970 from the Kennedy Space Center, Florida, and should have landed on the Moon. However, there was an explosion of an oxygen cylinder approximately 56 hours into the mission, forcing the spacecraft to circle the Moon and return directly to earth without landing on the Moon. So there was a massive forecast failure of its arrival time on the Moon. Indeed, not only did the spacecraft not land on the Moon at the predicted time, but it never landed on the Moon, so forecast errors are still increasing. What does this event tell us about the validity of the theory of moon shots, and the 'quality' of NASA's forecasting models that so badly mis-predicted the timing of the Moon landing?

Such models of space flight are based on Isaac Newton's laws of gravity and NASA's forecasting algorithms. Should we discard these as the forecasts were wrong? Certainly not. Indeed, NASA used both that gravitational theory and its forecasting algorithms to correctly track the subsequent motion of the spacecraft and bring the astronauts safely back to Earth. The forecast failure occurred due to an unanticipated event in the forecast period, and does not, and need not, by itself reject the forecasting model or the underlying theory from which that model was derived.

We should only reject a theory if it is supposed to give a complete and exhaustive description of all eventualities, leaving no place for 'unanticipated events'. But it is hard to imagine that this could be ever the case in a social science discipline. This contrasts with the universality of Einstein's equation, which would be disproved if there was a single irrefutable occurrence of an object traveling faster than the speed of light.[7]

In economics, the ability of forecasting to reveal poor models depends both on the properties of the data and on the structure of the model: good models can forecast poorly and bad models can forecast well. Of course, it is also true that good models can forecast well and bad models can forecast poorly, which makes it clear that forecast performance is not a discriminating criterion between good and bad models. Obviously, however, it does discriminate between good and bad forecasts! As the above example shows, there need be no connection between the validity, or verisimilitude, of a model, in terms of the 'goodness' of its representation of the economy, and any reasonable measure of its forecast accuracy. What does this imply? Well, it opens the door to using deliberately mis-specified models to forecast, which we go on to explore in the next chapter.

---

[7]In September 2011, the OPERA experiment appeared to show neutrinos traveling faster than the speed of light. Initially, neutrinos were claimed to have traveled the 731 km journey from CERN in Geneva to OPERA, in central Italy, some 60 nanoseconds faster than was possible. The anomaly is now generally regarded as being due to 'timing glitches'.

Chapter 8

Can we avoid systematic forecast failures?

> To expect the unexpected shows a thoroughly modern intellect.
> Oscar Wilde, *An Ideal Husband*, 1895.

The subtitle of this chapter could be 'what works, if anything?' In Chapter 7, we left our motorist contending with a collapsed bridge. If she continues to forecast her journey time *as if* the conditions surrounding her journey were essentially unchanged, her forecasts will tend to be systematically over-optimistic. Clearly the underlying model being used to forecast is no longer appropriate, assuming the 'best route' picked out by her sat-nav entails crossing the now closed bridge. Of course real-time traffic tracking devices might suggest greater congestion than usual, which will increase her expected journey time, but her actual journey time will still be longer than she forecast. So, having mis-forecast badly on the trip when the bridge collapsed, when faced with a similar journey to be undertaken in the future, how might she forecast its duration?

A simple strategy would be to set her forecast equal to that last *actual* journey time, or an average of recent journey times in general. This will not be a perfect forecast because journey times differ from day to day for a number of reasons (e.g., weather, weekday versus weekend traffic, etc.), some of which might have been accounted for in her existing 'model' for forecasting journey times. The effects of these factors will be lost when just using the previous time taken. Nevertheless, we can imagine situations where the neglect of these factors has a relatively minor effect on the quality of the overall forecast relative to automatically making an allowance in her 'model' for the detour required by the now uncrossable river. By setting the forecast to the actual time from the previous journey, the forecast embodies the impact on journey time of that detour. This requires that the next journey is comparable to the one previously undertaken, so we are assuming it's essentially the same journey: if so, it is likely to take a similar time.

In macroeconomic forecasting, the parallel is that next quarter's rate of inflation, or GDP growth etc. should be comparable to the current-quarter's rate, when any extraneous factors affecting the economy this quarter (e.g., a lower exchange rate, or increased taxes) are also in play next quarter.

Our motorist is now content—she is able to produce reasonably accurate forecasts. However, a moment's thought suggests that her contentment may be short-lived. Suppose she wishes to travel to another destination, say B. Clearly the actual journey time for A is not helpful in forecasting the journey time to B unless A and B are very close together. She knows her 'model' for forecasting journey time to A is performing poorly, but this tells her nothing about whether she can trust the model for forecasting the journey time to B. Whether she should trust the model will depend on whether the best route to B would try to take her across the fallen bridge.

So what have we learnt? Our motorist can avoid making systematic errors by the simple expedient of using her last journey time as the forecast, but this isn't perfect, and ignores knowledge that the motorist possesses which might be relevant (e.g., it's a school holiday so the roads will be quieter than usual). Before discussing the implications for macroeconomic forecasting, this lesson can be underscored by a consideration of the 'bus-stop game'.

The bus-stop game

Imagine that you are waiting at a bus stop, and in order to pass the time, you challenge your friend to a forecasting competition. The rules of the game are very simple. You aim to forecast when a student, who is also waiting at the bus stop, will leave. The game is that every 30 seconds you and your friend must each record a forecast for the next 30 seconds as to whether the student will have left. And to make the game more interesting, the one with most correct forecasts wins $10 from the other.

Now, you have the advantage of having read thus far in the book, and you decide to opt for a simple forecasting rule: you predict that, provided the student has not already left the bus stop, he will still be there in 30 seconds; and when he has left the bus stop, you predict he will be gone. This is analogous to our motorist forecasting that the duration of her next journey will be that of the last journey she undertook. Both are essentially 'no-change predictors'. The motorist's journey-time forecast is the same (i.e., no-change) relative to the last actual journey time. In the bus-stop game, the 'state of the world' is forecast to be what it was (no-change), specifically what was observed in the previous 30 seconds. In the economics literature this is known as a 'random-walk forecast', a simple model noted in Chapter 7.

However, your friend is an economist who takes the competition seriously, so he decides to use a causal model to forecast, based on his knowledge that students wait at bus stops to get on buses. Thus, his forecasting model states that, if no bus approaches, he forecasts the student will still be there, and, as a bus approaches, he forecasts the student will leave.

These are two different forecasting models, which we will call 'extrapolative' versus 'causal'. Do you or your friend win the $10? Five minutes elapse before the student leaves, so you are correct 10 times, then wrong once, but thereafter correct for ever. However, buses for four different destinations pass, and the student does not leave on any of them. Then his friend collects him on her motorcycle. Thus, your friend the economist is wrong four times in the five minute period, and if he refused to abandon his causal model, would remain wrong forever, as the student did not depart on a bus!

Congratulations on your $10. Now let's unpick this simple no-change predictor and see why it 'works'. Should we really give up on trying to provide causal forecasts of phenomena?

Risks and benefits of 'causal' models

The no-change predictor won the 'bus-stop' forecasting competition because an unanticipated outcome happened. By unanticipated we mean with reference to the causal model, which didn't allow for the possibility that students stand at bus stops for reasons other than catching buses. In these settings, causal models can mis-forecast badly. However, even if the student had been waiting for a bus, the no-change forecasts would still only have been wrong for the single period when the bus arrived and the student boarded. Consequently, the no-change forecasts would have been accurate in all but one period, and would still have beaten the causal model if the first few buses to arrive at the stop were not the correct buses for the student. Strictly from a forecasting perspective, where in addition we assume the costs of forecast errors are symmetric (that is, the costs of mistakenly assuming the student leaves, and of mistakenly assuming the student stays, are equal), we might be happy with the simple forecasting rule.

But it is easy to come up with counter-examples. Consider the need to decide whether or not to evacuate the inhabitants of a village close to a smoking volcano. Using a retrospective no-change predictor that 'the volcano will not explode' until it does, is completely useless, as it offers no advance notice. Thus, causal models which are forward-looking are an essential basis for forecasting in a policy environment, even if they are a risky way of forecasting in a non-stationary world.

Forecast failures reveal that we lack a full understanding of the process, signaling a need for deeper research, although we will continue to fail intermittently when new unexpected events happen (such as Brexit?). An important message of this book is that causal models can forecast well in 'normal times'. Of course, so do no-change forecasts, albeit usually with wider interval forecasts. If causal models were able to forecast shifts before they occurred, then the good performance would carry over to abnormal times too. However, in the presence of unanticipated shifts, forecasts must be adjusted rapidly after such events happen.

> To emphasize his recommendation for more research on forecasting, Hendry concluded his first discussion of the bus-stop game by remarking that 'when weather forecasters go awry, they get a new super-computer; when economists mis-forecast, we get our budgets cut'. Hendry and Ericsson, *Understanding Economic Forecasts*, MIT Press, 2001.

Causal, or structural, models permit policy analysis, seeking to answer such questions as to what would happen to output growth and inflation if the monetary authorities increased interest rates by, say, 2 percentage points. Such models can provide useful estimates of the effects of changes in policy variables without necessarily providing accurate forecasts of the future state of the economy. Of course the desirability of implementing any given policy change will depend on accurately forecasting what would otherwise eventuate. If causal models are to be competitive at *forecasting*, rapid adaptation to major changes in the economic system is essential, especially when those changes are themselves unpredictable. A serious criticism of historical forecast errors is how *systematic* they have been—not so much that the forecast errors were sometimes large.

For the United Kingdom, long sequences of under-prediction and over-prediction have been recorded, and have probably contributed to public mistrust in economic forecasting. Non-causal forecasting devices, such as no-change predictors, may help avoid systematic errors, but do so simply by adaptation to the most recent observations which eliminates tracking errors. Such devices do not provide knowledge about the future as they merely state that 'tomorrow will be the same as today', which it will be if nothing changes, but not otherwise.

Why might retrospective no-change predictors tend to work reasonably well for macro-forecasting in normal times? By analogy with the motorist using a no-change predictor for 'similar journeys', many macro-series that we might want to forecast are persistent. Take the rate of inflation as an example. The correlation between the rates of inflation in adjacent quarters is 0.95.[1] Consequently, next quarter's rate of inflation is very likely to re-semble the previous quarter's inflation rate, more so than the sample mean inflation rate, or the rate of inflation from ten years ago, for example. This property is shared by many economic time series, and, just as our motorist might be justified in using a no-change predictor for similar journeys, so might an economic forecaster. When there is an abrupt change, this will necessarily be missed, but, provided the changed state is itself reasonably persistent, then the no-change predictor will adapt and be back-on-track once it is conditioned on the newly changed value, mirroring the perfor-mance of the no-change predictor in the bus-stop game. We have already come across this phenomenon in a related guise in Figure 6.9 where the unexpected location shift was removed by differencing. The co-breaking shown in Panel (b) was achieved by subtracting the previous value from the present one (as opposed to that achieved in Panel (c) by subtracting another location shift). Using the previous outcome as the forecast works well till the shift occurs, misses for one period, then works well again after the shift. In the simple setting of a one-off location shift in an otherwise deterministic process, the previous outcome delivers complete adaptation. More generally, in a non-stationary stochastic world, recent outcomes may be the best available information about the next period.

Adaptation as forecasts go wrong

Adaptation relies on rapidly updating forecasting models to keep their forecasts on track. The no-change predictor is an adaptive forecasting de-vice. However, as we intimated in the discussion of the motorist using her last actual journey time, it will necessarily ignore knowledge that is likely to affect the outcome (for example, whether it is a weekday, or a weekend). A forecasting device which exhibits adaptability, without losing the poten-tial benefit of such knowledge, is called an intercept correction (IC), or add factor, to set the forecast 'back on track'. Previous forecast errors (or the latest error) are used to estimate the impact of whatever event is causing

---

[1] Calculated using the annual percentage change in quarterly UK consumer price inflation (CPI) for the period 1990:Q1 to 2017:Q2 (source: ONS MM23).

systematic mistakes, such as the collapsed bridge. Subsequent forecasts are then adjusted for the impact of this event by adding on the recent error as a correction. Returning to the issue raised in Figures 4.1(a) and (b) of whether A or B won, we can now resolve the question of whether the decision should have been different depending on forecasting the levels or the changes.

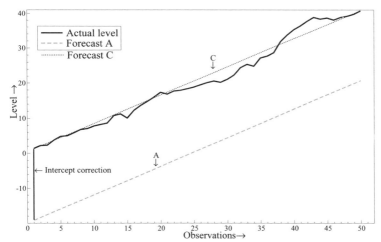

Figure 8.1: Forecast A amended by an intercept correction to forecast C.

Once the large first forecast failure has been observed, calculate the forecast error as the discrepancy between forecast A and the outcome at the forecast origin, as shown in Figure 8.1. Then this value can be used as an intercept correction for subsequent forecasts to offset the tendency of forecast A to under-forecast. The correction factor is roughly 20 units, and adding that to all later forecasts by A produces forecast C, which can be implemented before the later forecasts are made. This corrected forecast wins over B in levels, and had already won in changes since by construction, A and C produce identical forecasts of changes.

> Amusingly, if you had shown A's forecasts of *changes* to your boss, and
> he or she requested you to cumulate *those* to calculate the forecasts of
> the levels starting from the forecast origin value, then you would also get
> forecast C.

Intercept corrections can be viewed as a way of formalizing judgemental adjustments about the impact of extraneous events that are not included
in the forecasting model, as well as making an allowance for observed deficiencies, as in the example just given. Generally, of course, the forecast
will not under-estimate (or over-estimate) the actual value by the exact
same amount in each of a number of periods, so the forecast error in any
period will not provide a clean estimate of the required adjustment. In particular, the forecast error will include the realization of the random error
term in the model, which is not expected to persist, so an intercept correction will increase the forecast-error variance while correcting a possible
bias.

We describe forecasting models which *automatically* correct the forecasts in response to a location shift as exhibiting robustness after such
shifts. The no-change predictor is then a robust forecasting device. Intercept corrections offer robustness when based on recent errors. In practice, the real-time detection of events, such as the collapse of the bridge,
may not be immediately apparent from the forecast error *alone*, as a large
under-estimate might simply be bad luck. For example, the motorist might
happen to run up against a string of red lights, or temporary delays due to
roads blocked by delivery trucks. Assuming that future journey times will
take as long as the most recent will then result in over-predictions. Effectively, our motorist has mistakenly assumed that the series of unfortunate
one-off events that beset her latest journey are permanent so need to be
factored into future calculation. However, the motorist would immediately
know when the longer than expected journey was due to the closed-down
bridge which will take some months to repair.

This is an instance where our motoring analogy is less than perfect. In
the realm of macro-forecasting, whether a large forecasting error is due to
a discernible, persistent change may not necessarily be apparent till much

later. An advantage of an intercept correction is that the source of the failure need not be known. Unfortunately, applying an intercept correction when there has not been an underlying location shift will add noise to the forecast. Indeed, a large measurement error might initially appear to be the start of a location shift, but if revised away in the next period would have entailed a poor forecast.

Forecast robustification aims to use model forms that automatically and quickly move back on track after a location shift.

The models in Chapter 7 had the key characteristic that their forecasts reverted back towards the (historical) equilibrium of the model, so they were not robust after a shift in the equilibrium mean over the forecast period.

Rather than forecast-error correcting, in contrast to the adaptive device we have just discussed, they equilibrium correct, so converge back to the previous equilibrium, which exacerbates forecast errors when that equilibrium is out-dated.

Why does differencing work?

Figure 8.2 offers a visual intuition as to why robustification by differencing works, extending Figure 6.9 by also including broken trends, namely where the rate of growth shifts. These are stylized graphs so the vertical axis isn't important, but think of time on the horizontal axis, starting in month 1 through to 100 months later, and the series plotted is the mean of the data being forecast.

In Figure 8.2 Panel (a), imagine that the economy is running along quite steadily in equilibrium but suddenly, in month 50, there is a big upward shift and from then on the economy runs at a new equilibrium. Any model that was used to forecast from month 50 onwards, using the observations $1 - 49$, would extrapolate forward and assume the economy would remain at the past equilibrium level (i.e., 0) as shown by the dashed line. The shift would be missed and the next 50 months would suffer systematic

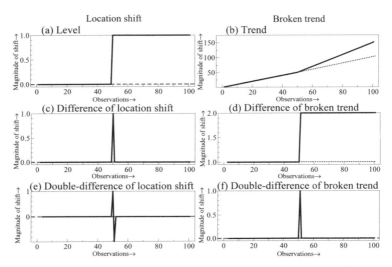

Figure 8.2: The effects of differencing a location shift and a broken trend.

forecast errors until the model was revised. Figure 6.3 showed the 'small' shift in the growth rate of UK GDP per capita after World War II that was only recently found by applying step indicator saturation, and its omission had previously distorted model estimates.

Now move to Figure 8.2 Panel (c) which plots the change in the series from Panel (a). For each value of the series in one month (e.g., 0 in month 25), subtract the value in the previous month (also 0 in month 24). When series (a) is constant, the difference is 0. The only point at which (c) is not 0 is at observation 50, where observation 50 minus observation 49 is one. Using series (c) to forecast by extrapolating forwards shows that the forecaster will be wrong in one month, as the shift in (a) was not anticipated, but after that the forecasts are back on track. No systematic mistakes are made. So, if there is a shift in the mean or equilibrium of a variable, differencing avoids a string of forecast mistakes. The 'bus-stop game' has a serious implication for settings where location shifts are unanticipated.

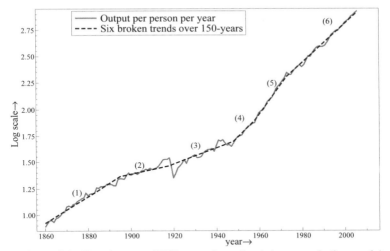

Figure 8.3: Trend rates of UK annual productivity growth (log scale).

All well and good, but what if the structural break is not a shift in the mean, but rather a shift in the trend rate of growth? A timely example of this phenomenon is the UK productivity slowdown following the financial crisis, possibly a change in trend rather than a temporary decline in productivity as in Figure 8.3. Figure 3.1 showed the historical pattern of GDP output per person per year, with six separate trends fitted to approximately 150 years (numbered as e.g., (3), etc.). The trend is different in each of these periods, being much faster at some times than others, and usually closely describing the data, although the data volatility is much higher over 1910–1960.

Figure 8.4 shows the dramatic impact on forecasts of different extrapolations of past trends. Panel (a) uses the last trend line over 1995 estimated up to 2007 to forecast the next 7 years. The 'flattening' in actual productivity growth is marked from 2008 onwards, so a forecast from that trend line is a bad description, revealing large and increasing forecast errors. Conversely, the Panel (b) graph in Figure 8.4 shows forecasts based on the

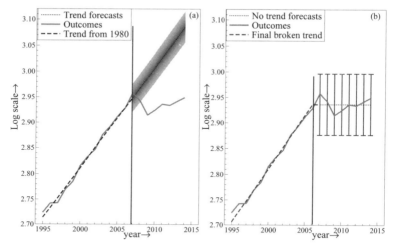

Figure 8.4: Potential forecasts assuming different trend behavior.

assumption of no trend growth, all of which happen to lie well within their error bars.

Figure 8.2 Panel (b) illustrated such a shift in trend, but where the economy increases its trend rate of growth at observation 50, as it did around 1960 in Figure 8.3. Forecasts from observation 50 onwards in Figure 8.2 (b) using the data up to month 49 will give the wrong trend prediction as shown by the dotted line. Not only that, but the forecast errors will worsen over time, as we also see in Figure 8.3. Forecasting models only have in-sample data available, so cannot predict a change in trend from past observations alone: another source of information is needed.

Let's try the same trick of differencing the broken trend to see if that helps. Figure 8.2 Panel (d) plots the change in the series in Panel (b), using the same method as above. When the trend is not changing, its difference will be constant. But the faster trend growth from month 50 onwards gives a different change in trend from that of the slower growth rate. How will our forecasts based on Figure 8.2 Panel (d) perform? Unsurprisingly (looking carefully at the Figure) they will be the same as the forecasts for Panel (a)! Systematic forecast mistakes will occur from month 50 onwards using the past differences, as the dotted line shows. But applying the same solution as in Figure 8.2 Panel (c), we difference that data again to obtain Panel (f). Now, we make a forecasting mistake at the point of the change in trend, but no systematic forecast errors after that. By 'double differencing' we have reduced the change in trend to an outlier, and forecasts will be back on track immediately after the shift.

Is there a cost to 'over-differencing'? What if the break was a shift in mean (i.e., Figure 8.2 Panel (a)) but we used a 'double-differenced model' to forecast? This results in the 'blip' shown in Panel (e), where two mistakes are now made, at observations 50 and 51. This blip will lead to two forecast errors when the break occurs, but the forecasts will be back on track two periods after the break. So the costs of over-differencing are minimal compared to the 50 forecast errors that would occur by not differencing at all and forecasting using Figure 8.2 Panel (b).

Table 8.1: Means, standard deviations (SDs) and RMSFEs of UK productivity forecast errors over 2009–2014.

	Mean error	SDs	RMSFE
Trend	−0.097	0.022	0.099
Intercept correction	−0.077	0.022	0.080
Difference ('robust')	−0.017	0.014	0.022

Table 8.1 records the means, standard deviations and square roots of the MSFEs, called root mean square forecast errors, denoted RMSFEs, for our UK productivity forecast errors over 2009–2014 by several methods. The trend extrapolation model fitted to data from 1984–2008 has the largest RMSFE, primarily from the near 10% overestimation of average growth, somewhat reduced if an intercept correction is estimated from the last residual at 2008, though really a trend correction would be needed as

the divergence grows over time. However, the RMSFE is just 0.022 from the differenced model—less than a quarter of the trend model's RMSFE—although it simply forecasts future growth as the mean over 1984–2008. That mean growth was around 1.7%, so the mean error of the robust model is −1.7% as no real growth occurred.

This principle of differencing is a method to remove the deterministic components of a forecasting model, by which we mean intercepts and trends. Deterministic terms capture the underlying equilibrium and growth rate of a variable of interest, so are fundamental to modeling, but can be catastrophic for forecasting when either component changes. The differencing principle can be applied to any model with an inherent equilibrium to which it corrects (which includes most model forms in economics) whilst retaining the important economic effects of a model such as policy parameters, feedback effects, or long-run relations. But buyer beware. If the object needing to be forecast is the level, a good performance forecasting the differences is not necessarily sufficient, as cumulating those differences may lead to an increasing divergence from the level.

Robustification can help

Robust forecasting models have proved to be successful in a policy context. In 2003, at the time of the ITV3 license-fee renewal, Hendry was asked by the UK communications industries regulator and competition authority, OfCom, to forecast discounted TV net advertising revenue (NAR) 10 years ahead. OfCom needed to calculate what renewal fee to charge ITV3 for the license to broadcast with advertising.

Forecasting 10 years ahead is no mean feat, but this is the relevant horizon for the license fee renewal, so some idea of advertising revenues at the 10 year horizon is essential, albeit discounted. There were many structural breaks during the years running up to the forecast origin, including the introduction of personal video recorders (PVRs), several new non-terrestrial TV channels, some with and some without advertising, and new Freeview channels, as well as both bar-code based and internet advertising, and possibly other changes. These shifts, which occurred just prior to the forecast origin in 2003, led to increased competition for advertising at the same time as audience fragmentation. Both demand and supply of TV advertising time were affected, and it was impossible to disentangle the consequences of such complex changes from just a few observations.

So how did Hendry proceed? He built a dynamic system comprising the real price per unit of TV advertising time, net advertising revenue, and audience reach to capture all the interactions between those variables, explicitly modeling both the short-run dynamics and long-run relationships, and modeling outliers near the forecast origin. This system was conditioned on aggregate economic variables including company profits, aggregate consumers' expenditure, inflation, etc. Think of this as the 'causal model'. Forecasts for the aggregate variables were taken from an external macroeconomic model and plugged into his system to compute the 10 year ahead forecasts for the key variables needed to calculate the fee. But this model was not sufficient given the structural changes occurring. Whilst a good model in-sample, Hendry then transformed the model by differencing it. This robustification retained the main causal effects of the model, which were essential for policy analysis, but removed the equilibrium embedded within the model. Consequently the forecasts over the 10 year horizon were not 'pulled back' to the in-sample equilibrium, but reflected the rapidly changing environment described above.

Let's look at the forecasts. Figure 8.5 records the forecasts of TV net advertising revenue for Total, Analogue and Multi-channel produced in 2003. Extrapolating the long-run trend predicts growing TV advertising revenue. In 2003, company profitability was high, there was a credit boom leading to growing consumers' expenditure, and inflation was low and stable. The benign conditions looked conducive to rising advertising revenue. But what about all the structural shifts noted above? Indeed, NAR was actually falling at the start of the millennium despite the favorable economic conditions, reflecting the influence of those unmodeled changes.

The differenced, or robust, model, showed a distinct downward trend for Analogue NAR over the decade ahead. Such forecasts led to a very different license fee than if the trend had just been extrapolated. Even for total NAR, the differenced forecasts show a distinct dip and a slower later growth rate. In 2016, net TV advertising revenue for the UK was £4.14bn,

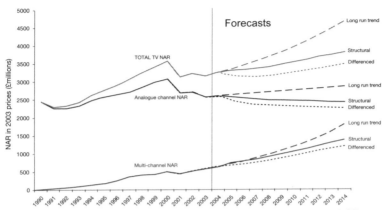

Figure 8.5: Forecasts of TV net advertising revenue: source OfCom.

which is approximately £2.83bn in 2003 prices.[2] The differenced 10 year ahead forecasts were much more accurate than trend extrapolation or the untransformed structural model. The robust model captured the structural break effects at the forecast origin, leading to predictions of falling real net advertising revenue, which is what happened over the next decade, albeit exacerbated by the (at the time) unforeseen Great Recession after 2008.

[2] See https://www.statista.com/statistics/236916/tv-net-advertising-revenue-in-the-uk/ for current data.

Chapter 9

How do we automatically detect breaks?

> Everything was happening so oddly that she didn't feel a bit
> surprised...
> Alice in Lewis Carroll, *Through the Looking-Glass and What
> Alice Found There*, London: Macmillan and Co., 1899.

In this Chapter, we consider the potential impact of in-sample shifts on out-of-sample forecasts. Although mean shifts during the forecast period will cause forecast failure irrespective of how well the model fits the data within sample, unmodeled in-sample shifts can also cause failure, as we illustrated with UK wage inflation. A possible example confronting our motorist of an in-sample shift would be a reduction in maximum speed, possibly from petrol shortages. Say motorway driving speeds had been reduced to 50mph, but her sat-nav still calculated journey times based on the earlier 70mph limit: this would lead to forecast failure but is clearly a form of shift that her forecasts could take into account.

Fortunately, there is a powerful, automatic method that can be used to account for in-sample shifts and outliers, introduced below in terms of how well it worked in a 'competition' for modeling food demand.[1] We cannot do anything about unforeseen future shifts, but can make an allowance for those which have already occurred.

In this econometric modeling competition in 1998, econometricians were asked to revisit an empirical model of US food expenditure, first examined by Nobel Laureate James Tobin in 1950. The extended sample consisted of annual data from 1929–1989. Many contributors found their models were non-constant over the inter-war and immediate post-war samples, and so dropped the earlier part of the sample and used post-war data alone. This would be akin to examining just the last epoch of the UK inflation data. One could get a fairly accurate estimate of the recent mean from such an approach, and use this along with estimated dynamics to forecast future food demand, or wage and price inflation, etc. But much is lost by this approach, as Figure 9.1 reveals. In every panel, the data variation before 1952, shown by the vertical line in Panel (a), is much greater than afterwards. Excluding past data reduces the variability of the sample, which in turn means that less precise estimates of the models can be achieved. Not only that, but such an approach casts doubt on the model's usefulness. If models are not constant across extensions of the sample, then they cannot represent the structure of the process under analysis. Consequently, they provide an unreliable tool for forecasting and policy as they are already known to have failed over some time periods.

Hendry approached the US food expenditure problem differently by choosing to model the whole of the available sample. But how to handle a dataset that looks so different over different periods? The important aspect that Hendry brought into play was to model the shifts. This led to a decades-long research agenda on modeling in-sample shifts and outliers that allows an empirical model to be based on the largest available dataset. There is no need to discard data because it 'looks different' or doesn't fit with the model estimated over a particular sub-sample. A good economic model should be able to represent all aspects of the data, including any distributional shifts in sample.

---

[1]See *Further Reading* for references. The 'competition' followed the Dodo's decision in Chapter 4, as the organizers declined to specify what outcome would qualify as 'winning'.

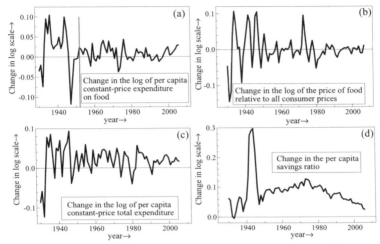

Figure 9.1: (a) change in the log of US per capita constant-price expenditure on food; (b) change in the log of US food prices relative to all consumers' goods prices; (c) change in the log of per capita constant-price total expenditure; (d) change in the per capita savings ratio.

So how did he do it? To investigate why other researchers dropped the early data, he added impulse indicators for all observations pre-1952. An impulse indicator takes the value of one for a single time period, say 1933, and is zero everywhere else. Such an impulse indicator makes a model fit perfectly for that observation, so eliminates the residual (model error) for 1933. The use of impulse indicators allows us to account for one-off effects by 'dummying them out'. The impulse indicators he added are an example of 'dummy variables'. Dummy variables are deterministic creations which take some numerical values for a pre-specified set of observations, but are zero at all other observations, like the variable in Figure 8.2 Panel (a). Dummy variables (including impulse indicators) are often used in economic models to account for events that are outside the standard economic forces, such as the effects of world wars, oil crises, or legislative changes, so have an effect over and above that accounted for by the model's explanatory variables.

Including impulse indicators for all observations pre-1952 allowed him to replicate the findings of the investigators who had dropped those earlier data points from their samples, yet to determine whether those earlier observations were markedly different from the later observations in an important sense. A war will dramatically change the economic relationships between variables, for example by restricting usual expenditure on food due to rationing, but the relationships holding 'in normal times' have not disappeared. Instead, 'extraordinary times' temporarily negate the standard economic forces and, if not handled, can contaminate what the data suggest about relationships. Impulse indicators eliminate outlying or contaminating observations from the model, allowing the standard relationships to be established. This allows all data to be used in modeling as 'extreme' data points like outliers are removed by impulse indicators.

Adding impulse indicators for every observation over 1929–1952 to remove that data period from the estimates of the model revealed three very large impulses corresponding to highly discrepant data points. Archival research then established that two of these 'outliers' were due to a US Great Depression food program and the third to post-war de-rationing: no surprise that such changes would have an impact on the demand for food. Then to check that his model fitted to the early data remained constant over the period from 1953 on, he included impulse indicators for all observations in this later period. That was a well-established test, so nothing new there. But in total, Hendry had included more variables plus impulse indicators than available observations, albeit in large blocks and not all at once. From these, he retained only the few indicators that removed the observations that were most discrepant relative to the food demand model. The resulting model with the usual economic determinants of food demand (food prices, per capita income, family size, etc.) plus impulse indicators for the food program and post-war de-rationing delivered a constant equation over the (then) whole sample.

Now for the clever part. We know when wars and legislative changes occurred, so we could add in indicators (or dummy variables more generally) for these events by hand, based on our institutional knowledge. But that may not be sufficient. There may be times that cannot easily be ascribed to known historical events but during which economic relationships nevertheless do temporarily alter. And, equally, there may be large events that we think must change the economic relationships but that turn out not to. For example, the savings ratio in Panel (d) has a huge spike during World War II over 1940–1946, from 'forced saving', but no indicators are required: the role of the savings ratio in the food demand model remains the same over the whole period. However, indicators would surely be needed if instead one was modeling the savings ratio. The solution to correctly determine these 'extraordinary observations' is based on using computer algorithms to detect the outliers in the data, a form of machine learning. Such algorithms allow for automatic detection, by quickly searching all possibilities for residuals that could constitute outliers. The approach is known as impulse indicator saturation.

Finding shifts by indicator saturation

Although it involves as many indicators as observations, we will use this setting to explain how we select variables that matter from a larger group of possible explanations. The approach allows for many possible explanations, then searches systematically through them to find the ones which receive the most support from the data.

Our approach is called 'General to Simple modeling' (*Gets*).

The approach considers a large number of potential explanations, and from them creates a general initial formulation.

From that, the algorithm selects a 'final model' that retains the variables which are the main influences in the sample of data for the variable we wish to forecast.

Present versions use an automatic selection algorithm.

This can be applied to select impulse and step indicators to capture past outliers or shifts as well as variables.

The final model is typically small, so is 'simple', compared to the 'general' we began with.

The technique of impulse indicator saturation creates an impulse indicator for every observation in the data set, but these are included in a model in feasible large blocks, and only those indicators which are statistically significant are retained. A model with a full set of indicators would fit perfectly, or *saturate*, the available observations. But the computer program *Autometrics* includes the indicators in batches, and checks whether any of the impulses within each batch are significant, so picks up discrepant observations relative to the model. By splitting the impulse indicators into batches and testing these, then combining the resulting retained indicators and testing again, the algorithm retains only the indicators that correspond to discrepant observations relative to the model. Note that it is relative to the model, not the data. An observation could look like an outlier when just observing the data, but could well be explained by the empirical model that has been estimated. This is why it is important to jointly select the model with the impulse indicators. Conversely, if outliers are not handled, very poor model estimates can result.[2] For example, food demand appears to *increase* with the price of food when outliers are ignored, with a price elasticity of $+0.11$, as against -0.15 once outliers are removed.

So far so good. We have an automatic method to pick up outliers over the in-sample period. The procedure works well, in the sense that, if there are no outliers, then very few of the indicators will be retained by accident, and the procedure has good power to detect observation that are actually discrepant.

In terms of the US food expenditure example, by including a few data-determined indicators in the model, both the inter-war and post-war regimes could be jointly modeled, an improvement on the models that discarded the earlier data. Since the original example, which was undertaken manually, the automatic approach has been applied to the same data and finds the same indicators. Success then, but how would this apply to the wage and price inflation data? Here, there aren't just discrepant observations, but persistent shifts in the mean of the data across the historical period. An extension of impulse indicator saturation provides the solution.

---

[2] See Hendry and Mizon (2011), 'Econometric modelling of time series with outlying observations', *Journal of Time Series Econometrics*, **3**(1).

Recall that an impulse indicator is a dummy variable that takes the value 1 for a given data point and 0 for all other observations, effectively setting the model residual to zero for that one observation. Instead, replace the impulse indicator with a step indicator that takes the value 1 for all observations up to a given observation, and zero from then on. This no longer eliminates one observation, but instead allows for the mean of the model to change over time by including step-shift dummies. The same computer algorithm can select step indicators, and the procedure has similar properties to that of impulse indicator saturation, so we have a method of modeling a changing mean over the sample period using data-based methods.

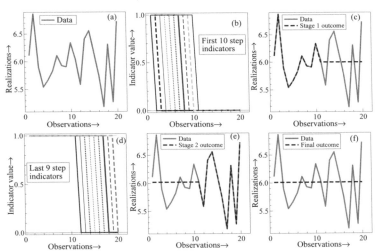

Figure 9.2: (a) 20 random observations; (b) the first 10 step indicators; (c) outcome after fitting to first 10; (d) last 9 step indicators; (e) outcome after fitting to last 9; (f) outcome after selecting significant indicators from either the first 10 steps or the last 9, or both blocks.

Although it may take a little more concentration to see how and why step indicator saturation works, we hope you will find it worth the effort.

Here the analogy is a new drug trial involving 20 randomly chosen individuals, split into 10 controls and 10 experimental subjects. The trial hopes to show that the drug raises the latter's health state. Now we need a small amount of probability. Drug trials have to decide what level of significance for the difference between the control and experimental treatments constitutes success that is unlikely to be due to chance. As there are only 20 subjects, that is often set at 5%, so that there is one chance in 20 that an apparent difference due to the new drug is just adventitious and actually does not work. Success is then a difference with a much smaller probability of occurring by chance.

Figure 9.2 Panel (a) plots the pre-trial measures of the data, organized by 'control' (in panels (a)–(c)) then 'experimental' (in (d) and (e)): the data here are of course just artificial computer generated random numbers. To check there is no chance mean difference between the groups, we first apply step indicator saturation to this pre-trial data in two blocks, checking for the significance of any of the first 10 indicators added as a block, then the last 9 (the 20th is just a string of 1s so is the same as the intercept and hence is not needed). Panel (b) shows the, admittedly uninteresting, plot of the 10 step indicators: the first starts at 1 and ends at 2, the last still starts at 1 but ends at 10. Panel (c) shows the fit when all 10 are included: a perfect match for the first 10 data points, and just a mean for the rest of the data. If we only keep those of the first 10 step indicators that are statistically significant, here using automatic model selection, no indicators are retained.

Next, Panel (d) records the last 9 indicators, and, as before, Panel (e) confirms the perfect fit to the second group. The outcome of retaining significant indicators from both the first 10 steps and the last 9 is shown in Panel (f): no steps are found, and just the overall mean (the intercept) is retained, so the two groups do not differ at the start.[3]

Finally, the trial is completed and the results are in: these are shown in Figure 9.3. We have used the same observations as in Figure 9.2, with the last 10 increased by 1 to highlight the changes. In Panel (g), the first

---

[3] Step indicators can also capture outliers, by two successive steps having equal magnitude but opposite sign values, such as $+2$, -2, so all the steps of the second indicator except the last one cancel—which is an impulse.

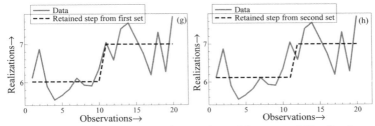

Figure 9.3: Same 20 random observation with a step shift of unity start-ing at observation 11; (g) selecting from the first 10 step indicators; (h) selecting from the last 9 step indicators.

10 step indicators have been included and any indicators significant at 5% or better are shown—in fact just the tenth step indicator was retained and reveals a sharp difference between the control and experimental mean val-ues. Actually, the increase in the mean between the groups is more sig-nificant than 1 in 1000, so is not due to chance, which we know is true here.

Panel (h) shows what happens when we select from the last 9 step indicators. As can be seen, step 11 is selected as the best approximation given the indicators available to the algorithm, but is still significant at almost the 1 in 1000 level. The key stage is to combine the findings from the two blocks and select the significant indicators, at which point step 11 is eliminated, leaving Panel (g) as the overall, and correct, outcome. Now we are the first to admit that an easier way to analyze this data is just to calculate the difference between the means of the two groups, which gives the same answer, but the aim here is to explain in a simple context how step indicator saturation works—and demonstrate that it does so despite having as many steps as observations.

Figure 9.4 records the mean shifts that step indicator saturation finds for UK wage inflation over the last century and a half, along with the mean of the full sample. If we were to forecast wage inflation using a model which embedded the full-sample average (the dotted line), we would pre-dict a higher inflation rate in the future than if we were to use the shifting

mean, shown by the dashed line. We don't have the outcomes so we don't
know which would produce more accurate forecasts, but it doesn't stretch
the imagination to think of the more flexible mean being better placed to
predict future outcomes. The wrong equilibrium in-sample would lead to
forecast failure out-of-sample even if the equilibrium were to remain constant out-of-sample. As it happens, the two possible forecasts are quite
close, and indeed since 1992 the overall and local means are the closest
they have been for more than a century.

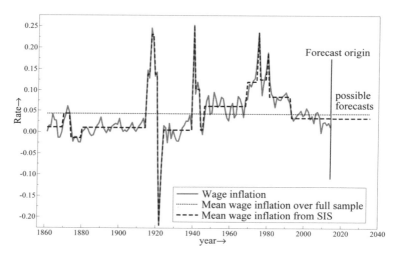

Figure 9.4: UK wage inflation over the last century and a half with outliers
and step shifts selected by step indicator saturation (SIS).

One way to think about what step indicator saturation is doing is to
recognize that it is simply finding what the mean would have been had
only the shorter sample been available. For example, consider the period
from 1860 to 1914: the mean was roughly zero. The *later* calculation of
the full-sample mean from 1860 of just over 4% pa is a poor representation
of that period's equilibrium, as shown by the gap between the dotted and

dashed lines before World War I. The inter-war years also have a mean inflation rate of near zero, so are close to the pre-war period. However, the mean from 1860–1922 is 1.8%, so if the deviant war inflation was not removed (which step indicator saturation achieves), the mean would be systematically wrongly calculated. For a successful forecast, it is imperative that the in-sample equilibrium is correctly modeled. Impulse and step indicator saturation provide an effective method of achieving this. But that is not the whole story. Even if the model has the correct in-sample mean, shifts in the equilibrium in the forecast period will still cause forecast failure: using the mean up to 1945 to forecast the next few years or, worse still, further into the future, would have seen considerable forecast failure.

The issue of biases in forecasts was discussed in Chapter 4, and impulse indicator saturation can be used to estimate these. A sequence of large negative forecast errors followed by a sequence of large positive forecast errors that together entailed an overall mean of zero would suggest an unbiased forecast. However, impulse indicator saturation would deliver some large negative indicators then some large positive ones to reveal a problem. SIS would summarize such a result by a negative then a positive step as a more parsimonious description. In both cases, the 'average' is zero, rather like the joke about a statistician being at a comfortable temperature on average with their head in a fridge and feet in an oven.

Chapter 10

Can we forecast breaks before they hit?

It is far better to foresee even without certainty than not to foresee at all.

Henri Poincaré, in *The Foundations of Science*, New York: The Science Press, 1913.

Our unlucky driver has experienced all sorts of obstacles and delays en route, but she breathes a sigh of relief as the traffic is finally flowing freely on her way to her destination. However, a glance at her sat-nav on the dashboard of her car indicates congestion on the road ahead from an accident. The satellites orbiting the earth not only detect our driver's location and speed, but the location and speed of other drivers as well. This information is overlaid onto road maps and the congestion down the road is anticipated by our driver. The sat-nav not only informs our driver of the impending traffic jam, but it also tries to find faster alternative routes. In effect, the additional information coming from the satellites enables our driver to temporarily alter the map, penciling in the blockage ahead. The information gathered by the GPS on the speed of cars on various possible routes is contemporaneous, so the forecast of our driver's journey time is updated and should be more accurate, but is still only a forecast. As our driver heads down an alternative route, her journey time will depend on how many other drivers choose the same alternative route causing the effects of the congestion to spill over onto her new route. Provided not too many other drivers decide to divert to that particular route, she will have forecast the break ahead—and managed to avoid it.

Technology has improved over time. Perhaps the earliest incarnation of the sat-nav may have been the stable boys at staging posts, reporting on delays to the mail coaches. The car radio enabled drivers to listen to the traffic reports on the radio before deciding on the appropriate route, which relied on drivers phoning in to their local radio station and reporting on the level of traffic they were experiencing. A more advanced solution for larger cities was to fly helicopters overhead to see where the traffic was building up. The modern technology of GPS has further increased the information set, thereby improving forecasts of the journey duration in real time. We can hope that better forecasts have led to shorter journey times, but instead may just have led to more traffic.

Wonderful, you might say. Our driver can phone her friend and update him on her arrival time, which should be reasonably accurate. But, before we congratulate ourselves on improving our forecasts, remember that we have not managed to forecast the event that led to the congestion. The accident itself was not predicted. We are merely updating our forecasts as new information arrives. In this Chapter, we ask what it would take to forecast the economic equivalent of the accident that caused the congestion. Structural breaks must have causes, so if we could ascertain those causes *in advance*, then presumably we could forecast the looming breaks? Perhaps the car involved in the accident had a bald tire, or there had been a recent downpour and the roads were wet and slippery. Or perhaps the subsequent police investigation would fail to uncover a single, specific cause, and the official reason would be recorded as human error? By analogy, it might not be an easy matter to unravel the causes of an economic break even after the event, let alone ahead of time. Forecasting breaks may be a tall order, but at least we might be able to forecast the effects of the shifts as they progress, much as our motorist is able to update her forecast as her journey progresses, and take action accordingly.

What would we need to know?

What would we need to know in *principle* to forecast structural breaks in the economic system? Doubters may scoff, given the poor *practical* forecasting performance in recent years: in Chapter 7 we mentioned the failure to forecast the Great Recession, the key economic event of the 21st century (thus far!). Nevertheless, we might at least be able to isolate the reasons why it is likely to be so difficult in practice to predict sudden shifts. Moreover, economists are not alone in attempting to forecast abnormal events in complex systems. After all, some major volcanic eruptions have been successfully forecast several hours before they occurred. Seismic monitoring along with satellite radar interferometry offer a route for prediction. Earthquake prediction is more difficult, but advances are being made. So why not in economics? We face 'economic earthquakes' such as financial crises, oil crises, political shocks, etc. What would it take to predict these?

First, the break would need to be predictable. There needs to be an information set on the basis of which the break could be predicted. This is obvious, as is the converse, that unpredictable breaks cannot be forecast. If the accident was due to a car's faulty brakes failing, which were known to be worn, then on an information set that included knowledge of the state of the brakes, the accident was predictable. If the accident that caused the congestion ahead was due to a driver suffering a heart attack behind the wheel, we might be inclined to say the accident and resulting congestion is unpredictable. Of course that heart attack might be predictable to a cardiologist who had recently examined our unfortunate driver, but would not have been so to our motorist. We do not need to concern ourselves with philosophical musings on whether anything is truly without cause.

If the break is predictable on a certain information set, the second requirement is that the information underpinning that predictability is known. The driver with the failing brakes needed to visit the garage and have his brakes tested before taking to the open road. Or the driver who had a heart attack would have needed to be aware that he was at risk.

The third requirement for forecasting breaks is that the relevant information is available in advance, that is, at the forecast origin. It is of no use to the driver with the failing brakes that the mechanic who recovers his car after the accident informs him that his brake pads were badly worn. He needed the information before he set out if he were to make use of that knowledge. Consider the 2007–2009 financial crisis. Some aspects of the crisis had antecedent causes such as sub-prime loans, moral-hazard-driven risk-taking, high leverage, increasing unsecured credit outstanding, growing income inequality, etc. Other contributory causes depended on policy decisions which could have been made differently, and may not have been predictable *ex ante*. For example, letting Lehmann Brothers go bankrupt was a major negative shock, whereas earlier Bear Stearns was merged with JP Morgan, and later many of the Organisation for Economic Co-operation and Development (OECD)'s largest financial institutions were bailed out. Consequently, some relevant information on the possible causes existed, and may even have been available at the time. However, important aspects such as agency problems and massive off-balance-sheet loans only became widely known later.

The fourth requirement is that there is a way of formalizing the diverse factors as a reliable early-warning system. That is, one needs a forecasting model that appropriately weights together the forecast-origin information. For example, the motorist may have been told that his brakes are just on the legal limit and will need replacing soon, that there may be black ice on untreated roads, but on the plus side he is planning to travel early in the morning, when there are likely to be few cars on the road. He will need a way of weighting the diverse and sometimes conflicting pieces of information if he is to reliably predict the chances of having an accident. His decision will also depend on his attitude to risk.

The fifth requirement is closely related and requires an operational method for selecting the forecasting model. In economics, there are a number of competing approaches to selecting forecasting models and what form those models should take.

In the motoring example, our driver might ask the mechanic to check not just the brake pads, but also the steering, suspension, engine, wheels, tires, and seatbelts. An algorithm could include all these possible causes of accidents across many cars and search through them to see which are most likely to cause an accident, using this model to predict the probability of an accident for our driver waiting at the garage having her car checked.

An alternative approach might be to construct an index (or a small number of indices) which leads the state of the economy, as measured by the growth of real GDP, for example, then uses this index to forecast the variable of interest. This is generally known as a factor model, because the index (or factor) is meant to distill the common movements in a large number of variables. As an example, there has been much interest in Financial Conditions Indices or FCIs. The current values of financial variables typically include information about the future state of the economy: they are said to be forward looking. An FCI attempts to aggregate the forward-looking information for a wide range of financial assets. The Financial Crisis which began in August 2007 in the US and preceded the Great Recession has led to reassessments of the value of FCIs. In practice, it is possible to use a hybrid of these approaches, that is, general-to-specific selection, *Gets*, on a set of variables which include factors.

So in an ideal world we will have a break that is predictable, with information relevant to that predictability available in advance, and a good model that uses the information appropriately to forecast the breaks. Even then, the sixth requirement is that the forecasts are reasonably *precise*. It is no good if the mechanic, after testing the brakes, tells the driver that he predicts there is a possibility of their failing, but that this could occur at any point within the next 25,000 miles, and may or may not be severe. If forecasting models have very wide margins of error for the occurrences, timings, signs, and magnitudes of breaks, then they cannot be used effectively, and with too great an uncertainty range would probably be ignored.

> The British, he thought, must be gluttons for satire:
> even the weather forecast seemed to be some kind of spoof,
> predicting every possible combination of weather for the next
> twenty-four hours without actually committing itself to any-
> thing specific.
> David Lodge, *Changing Places*, Secker & Warburg, 1975.

Along with precision, we require that the forecasts are *accurate*. If the mechanic reports that there is a 15% probability of an accident due to the brake pads failing if they are left unchanged, a risk-loving driver might be willing to take her chances. But if the mechanic is wrong, and the actual probability is as high as 50%, the driver who risked not changing their brakes may well have made a different decision and prevented an accident. Reasonably accurate forecasts are essential. As Paul Samuelson has been quoted, 'the stock market has predicted nine of the past five recessions!'[1]

If all the requirements for forecasting a break were satisfied, a successful forecast would avoid the forecast failures evident in Figure 7.5, for example, when positive growth is being forecast even as the US economy contracts during the Great Recession. But since the break is likely to evolve over time, we would also need methods for forecasting outcomes as the break progresses, as well as to signal the return to 'normal times', which in this instance would constitute the resumption of growth in real GDP. It is helpful to depict breaks as sudden shifts in means, as step changes that occur at specific dates. But economies have their own dynamics and events unfold over time. As an example, a sudden tax change will have an immediate effect at implementation (and possibly an anticipatory effect in advance of its being implemented). It will then feed through to savings decisions, and hence aggregate expenditure more slowly, perhaps over the course of a year or two. So, having successfully predicted a break, we now need to forecast the aftermath. In the motoring context, in the aftermath of the accident the extent of traffic congestion on neighboring roads will change, depending on how busy they were initially, and whether they are main roads or side roads, for example. All of these will need to be included in our driver's forecast.

Finally, forecasts may themselves change the distributions of future outcomes. Let's imagine that our driver opted for getting her brake pads replaced when she visited the garage, and when she was on the road the next day she needed to do an emergency stop. Her car halted successfully and the accident was avoided. So there was no structural break due to an accident caused by a failure of the car's brakes. But the mechanic had forecast that the accident was likely with the car's original brakes, hence the driver opted to replace her brake pads. The successful forecast

---

[1] Cited by Deborah Owen and Robin Griffiths, *Mapping the Markets: A Guide to Stockmarket Analysis*, Bloomberg Press, 2006, p.16.

of the mechanic changed behavior to prevent the accident. Evaluating the forecast *ex post*, an accident was predicted but no accident occurred. This apparent mis-prediction is due to a conditional forecast. Forecasts are made conditional on a certain set of circumstances. The probability of an accident is determined given the current condition of the car. If the forecast causes actions to be taken which change those circumstances, and result in a good outcome, then the forecast has proven valuable. Because the accident was averted, it was not observed.

Similarly in economics, we cannot see calamities which were nipped in the bud by a timely policy response, such as a reduction in interest rates to prevent the economy going into recession. The fact that economic outcomes may be influenced by forecasts sets the economist and policy maker apart from the weather forecaster, who has no effect on the weather, and complicates the job of forecasting and assessing the quality of economic forecasts, a difference emphasized by Sir John Mason, then director–general of the Met Office, and Nobel Laureate Amartya Sen commenting on Hendry.[2] While agreeing with Mason, we cannot help but add another quote:

> Though he did not know it, Rob McKenna was a Rain God. All he knew was that his working days were miserable and he had a succession of lousy holidays. All the clouds knew was that they loved him and wanted to be near him, to cherish him, and to water him.
> Douglas Adams, *So Long, and Thanks for All the Fish*, Pan Books, 1984.

Forecasting the Great Recession

The upshot of the previous section is that it is perhaps not surprising that the Great Recession in the US was not forecast in advance, and it took forecasters a while to catch on even when the recession was in full swing. This much is clear from Figure 7.5. It so happens that forecasters were not helped by the official early releases of GDP figures. We know from

---

[2]http://rspa.royalsocietypublishing.org/content/royprsa/407/1832/25.full.pdf.

Chapter 3 that official data are uncertain: early estimates are subject to revision. Table 10.1 shows the current-quarter forecasts along with the advance (first) and the most recent estimates for the period 2007:Q4 to 2009:Q3. The current-quarter forecasts are forecasts made in the middle of the quarter being forecast. So, for example, the 2007:Q4 forecast would have been made around November 15th, and is a forecast of the rate of growth in the fourth quarter relative to the third quarter (annualized). The forecasts are survey expectations, namely the median of the individual respondents' forecasts.[3] These are often called nowcasts despite being made in advance of (at least part of) the target. The forecasters missed the 2.7% contraction in the economy which occurred in 2008:Q1, as well as the near 2% fall in 2008:Q3, blithely expecting the economy to expand by 1.15%. Remember these are nowcasts of what is happening at the time: one might think there would have been ample information that the economy was not going well. But notice we have treated the most recent data as 'actual values': the early estimates released by the statistics agency also missed what was going on, so perhaps we are being overly hard on the forecasters who based their forecasts on misleading forecast origin values.

Table 10.1: Forecasts and uncertain initial data

	Forecast	First	Most recent
2007:Q4	1.54%	0.64%	1.44%
2008:Q1	0.67%	0.60%	−2.70%
2008:Q2	0.21%	1.89%	2.00%
2008:Q3	1.15%	−0.25%	−1.91%
2008:Q4	−2.94%	−3.80%	−8.19%
2009:Q1	−5.19%	−6.14%	−5.43%
2009:Q2	−1.53%	−1.02%	−5.39%
2009:Q3	2.44%	3.53%	1.31%

---

[3]The US Survey of Professional Forecasters (SPF), available at https://www.philadelphiafed.org/research-and-data/real-time-center/survey-of-professional-forecasters/.

The first time that the forecasters would have looked at the first estimate for the previous quarter and seen a decline in output would have been 2008:Q4. When they made their nowcasts of 2008:Q4 they would have been aware for the first time that the first estimate of the previous quarter showed a decline, albeit only a modest decline of a quarter of a percentage point. The nowcast for 2008:Q4 under-predicted the magnitude of the decline by about 1% point *on the basis of the initial release*, but was over 5% shy of the latest estimate of the decline in 2008:Q4!

We have considered the US, and survey expectations. A similar story could be told of the European Central Bank's nowcasts of euro area GDP.[4]

The 2004 Indian Ocean tsunami

As an example of forecasting structural breaks in a field outside of economics, consider the Boxing Day 2004 Indian Ocean tsunami. It was caused by an undersea earthquake off the west coast of Sumatra. In turn, that earthquake was triggered by a tension release at a subduction zone. Understanding how earthquakes reduce stress in a rupture zone, but increase stress in other parts of a fault, makes such events potentially predictable. Unfortunately, there was no relevant information for predicting the Sumatra earthquake at the time, so the cause was not predictable with the information available. However, once the earthquake had started a tsunami, its impact when it hit land could have been predicted by using information on its location, initiation, speed, and force of the shock wave. There are technologies in place for the detection, measurement, and real-time reporting of tsunamis. In fact a satellite, Jason-1, crossed the site of the tsunami wave front 2 hours after it commenced and recorded its existence by altimetry, hence well before it struck many of the areas devastated later that day, so a forecast was potentially possible, but the data were not analyzed till several days later. Following the earlier example set by the

---

[4]Geoffrey Kenny and Julian Morgan (2011), 'Some lessons from the financial crisis for the economic analysis', Occasional Paper 130, European Central Bank (ECB) report a 'clear failure to capture the period of exceptional macroeconomic weakness in the fourth quarter of 2008 and the first quarter of 2009' (p. 13).

Pacific Ocean tsunami warning system, one is also now in place around the Indian Ocean.

After discovering that a tsunami has started, there needs to be a method for selecting a forecasting model of its evolution, based on physical theory incorporating whatever data is delivered by the tsunami warning system in place. Once tsunamis are accurately measured, the precise timings and locations of impacts are predictable within fairly small intervals. These may still vary with the detailed seabed and shore topography, but this variation is small, and doubtless forecast-error bands could be designed to reflect some unmodeled features, increasing the intrinsic uncertainty. Given the potentially huge wave surges, the only sure defense against loss of life is evacuation to higher ground.

So forecasting breaks is feasible and there is evidence of success in fields outside of economics. As yet, the evidence of success within economics is sparse, so we will consider the next best alternative: that our forecasting models missed the break, but can adapt quickly as the effects of the break filter through the economy.

Two information sets

We failed to forecast an accident on the road ahead. But can we forecast how the resulting congestion will build up and then gradually dissipate on the surrounding roads? Often, that is possible. When unpredictable breaks occur in economics, is there potential for more rapidly adapting our forecasts than at present? One approach that holds promise is to distinguish between two separate information sets. One is the set of 'regular' forces that have some degree of constancy in their effects over time. So, in our driving analogy, this set would be factors such as the volume of traffic on the road, the type of road, weather conditions, the time of day, etc. The second information set relates to the causes of sudden shifts, for example, the worn brake pads or the risk of a heart attack. Partitioning the information enables us to build models based on the regular forces that hold for the majority of the time and use the additional information on sudden shifts to adjust the forecasting model, either by an add factor or switching to a different model, or allowing for adjustment to a new equilibrium. For the model of US food demand, Chapter 9 showed that regular forces can shine through in economics once contaminating influences are neutralized.

To make this idea of two information sets more concrete, let's consider a few examples. There is a large body of literature examining the determinants of civil wars. Paul Collier and Anke Hoeffler suggest there may be one set of forces that leads to the outbreak of a civil war, such as countries having had a war in the recent past, or reliance on a precious resource such as diamonds or oil, or low income growth, but a different set of factors that facilitate its continuation, such as increased poverty, political grievances, or the ability to recruit armed forces.[5] This suggests that two information sets could prove useful in modeling both the probability of an outbreak of civil war and its likely duration.

As another example, we return to modeling the demand for money first illustrated in Chapter 2.[6] In normal times, the demand for money can be modeled as depending on current and lagged prices, incomes, and the opportunity costs of holding money versus alternative assets. This model successfully captured the evolution of UK money demand before 1984, when the Finance Act that year stimulated a jump in interest-bearing sight deposits. The policy change shifted the opportunity costs of holding money, and altered money demand relative to the prevailing levels of the other economic determinants. The economic model was still correct, but the definition of the opportunity cost of holding money had suddenly shifted. Thus, the normal economic information set remains unchanged, whereas the second information set includes knowledge of the legislative change affecting taxes, which is key to allowing the forecasting model to be updated *ex post* and to generate more accurate forecasts for subsequent periods. Figure 2.7 demonstrated how great an improvement can result from doing so.

Finally, whether a specific break is predictable or not depends on the information available at the time. As discussed in Chapter 2, an observer

---

[5] 'Civil war', Chapter 22 in T. Sandler and K. Hartley (eds), *Handbook of Defense Economics*, Elsevier, 2007.

[6] See Hendry and Ericsson (1991), 'Modeling the demand for narrow money in the United Kingdom and the United States', *European Economic Review*, **35**, 833–886.

on the Moon with suitable equipment could have predicted Captain Cook's 'discovery' of New Zealand and his meeting the surprised Māori. But even then the observer may still not have forecast the discovery if it was a cloudy day, as the trajectory of the *Endeavour* could not have been followed by an optical telescope (but could perhaps by an 'x-ray' type). Alternatively, if a hidden underwater rock wrecked the vessel between the outside observer's forecast and Cook's arrival, the forecast would have failed from an unanticipated 'break'. In fact, *Endeavour* experienced that problem off Cape Tribulation as Cook approached northern Australia, hitting a coral reef that nearly sank his ship. Hence, the observer must have information that is relevant and available at the forecast origin, along with an appropriately selected model embodying the information, such that the forecasts of Captain Cook's arrival are usefully accurate (e.g., sudden strong gusts of wind do not blow the ship off course). The next chapter considers a possible role for non-linear models after missing breaks, but helping forecasting models adapt quickly.

Captain Cook was a trailblazer in navigation techniques, and used sextants, lunars, and the latest Harrison chronometer.[7] He would have had measures of latitude and longitude in his information set, and used this to forecast the path of *Endeavour*. But the outside observer with an accurate map of the South Pacific in their information set and local weather forecasts would still be better able to predict Cook's arrival on land.

---

[7] See Dava Sobel, *Longitude*, Penguin, 1995.

Chapter 11

Can we improve forecasts during breaks?

> 'Yes, all his horses and all his men,' Humpty Dumpty went on. 'They'd pick me up again in a minute, they would!'
> From Lewis Carroll, *Through the Looking-Glass and What Alice Found There*, London: Macmillan and Co., 1899.

By definition, a break is a sudden shift, so is bound to be difficult to predict. Forecasting early on during a break that is not completed instantaneously may offer a higher likelihood of success, so we now consider some examples trying to do so. First, we consider a break that follows a trajectory over a number of periods, which offers hope of estimating its progress at an early stage to forecast its later development. Next, we describe non-linear adjustment, namely changing more rapidly the larger the break, then note the possibility that breaks may follow a pattern that can be modeled, switching between several 'regimes', such as fast and slow for example. Breaks occur in many disciplines, so we also look at forecasting the damages caused by hurricanes, and the recovery of global temperatures after large volcanic eruptions.

Illustrating forecasting during a break

Figure 11.1 shows a deterministic break that climbs steadily from zero to unity. Every aspect of this illustration is designed to make it as easy as possible to forecast the trajectory that the break will take. We let the shape of the break function be known to one forecaster (but not others), although the actual numerical values of the formula determining the rate of climb are not known and have to be learnt as the break evolves.

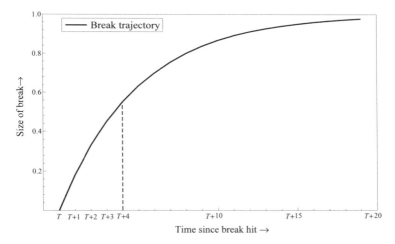

Figure 11.1: An artificial break function.

We will consider four methods of forecasting the break for the first 4 periods, all one step at a time, denoted $T + 1, \ldots, T + 4$, updating information about the break evolution as it proceeds. We measure their success by their mean squared forecast errors (MSFEs), which are reported in Figure 11.2. The first approach is just to ignore the break, called the unadjusted model, so the changes due to the break are simply forecast to be zero. The resulting MSFEs for the next four periods are shown by the thin dashed line, and increase steadily, being far higher than any other method: any attempt to forecast the path of the break is better then none.

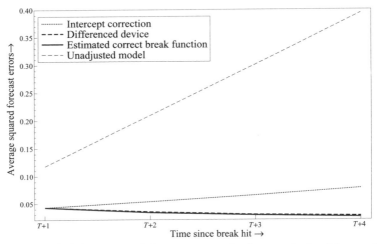

Figure 11.2: Mean squared forecast errors for four methods of forecasting during the break in Figure 11.1 over the first 4 periods.

Second worst is to use an average intercept correction, namely one that first uses the 1-step error, then the average of the first- and second-step errors and so on. This is shown as the dotted line, and is one of our methods here since it is less volatile than just a 1-period intercept correction after a location shift, and the second forecaster using it may not know that the break has the shape in Figure 11.1, and assumes it is a step shift. Next, the MSFEs for the differenced device we discussed in Chapter 8 are shown as the thick dashed line. Surprisingly, although the differenced method was designed for forecasting after a location shift, it also does remarkably well for the break in Figure 11.1, and its MSFEs fall as the horizon increases. Indeed, they are very close to the MSFEs of the estimates of the correct break function, shown as a solid line, which would usually be infeasible. Overall, the results are encouraging for forecasting during breaks, especially by the feasible robust approaches which require much less knowledge about the shape of the break function.

A possible role for non-linear models

So what are non-linear models and why are they needed? The break function shown in Figure 11.1 is clearly not linear, so requires a non-linear model to capture it. More generally, non-linear models allow relationships between variables to differ at different levels. This may be relevant when trying to forecast a shift, but is likely to be more useful in practice when forecasting after a break has occurred, because variables may no longer respond to each other in the way they did previously. Thus, adapting quickly in the aftermath of a break to the economic system may often require the use of non-linear models. In much of economics, models assume a linear relationship between variables, or between the natural logarithms of the variables, but a more non-linear form might be preferable for some links. As we have noted several times so far, breaks can be abrupt and often are not anticipated, making them exceptionally difficult to forecast. However, many sciences such as volcanology and geophysics have made advances in doing so, in areas where such events were historically sometimes attributed to angry gods rather than natural forces that might be understood. The breaks we focus on are location shifts, but we also allow for the possibility that such abrupt switches may be approximations to changes that unfold rapidly, rather than instantaneously.

As an illustration both of a non-linear form and an attempt to describe a break after it has started, Figure 11.3 shows the interest rate paid on UK checking accounts for the 20 quarters after the 1984 Finance Act (solid line, rescaled to lie between zero and unity). That interest rate was zero before the Act, then its increase was initially slow before rising rapidly over 2 to 7 quarters later. The dotted line is a step indicator approximation, treating the change as a single location shift, fitted after the event. The approximation is certainly better than ignoring the shift, but is not great and, in practice, several step indicators would probably be selected as an improved approximation.

The dashed line is an exponential curve approximation which captures the upswing quite closely. Had one known the form of such a curve at the start of the period, reasonable forecasts of the evolving break would have been feasible, although it can be difficult to estimate such non-linear

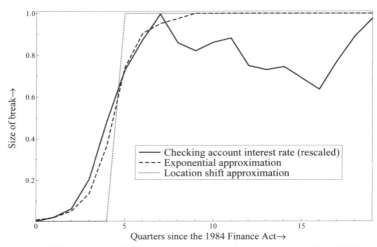

Figure 11.3: An artificial exponential function and a location shift as approximations to the interest rate paid on UK checking accounts for the 20 quarters after the 1984 Finance Act.

formulations sufficiently precisely to help until well into the break. Nevertheless are there methods that seek to do so.[1]

Missing breaks, but adapting quickly

Remember the straight line on Figure 1.4 in Chapter 1 approximating stopping distances that in fact rise non-linearly with speed? Using a linear approximation could lead to serious accidents at high speeds (and we worry that it may well do so in reality). Similarly, linearity would require that if individuals in the top decile of the income distribution save 10% of their income, individuals in the bottom decile would also have to save 10% of

---

[1]Smooth-transition multiple-regime models are one possibility: see Granger and Timo Teräsvirta, *Modelling Nonlinear Economic Relationships*, Oxford University Press, 1993.

their income. If an increase in the excess demand for goods and services by 1% pushes up inflation by approximately 1%, this proportionality would need to hold for any level of inflation.

As an economic example, imagine if prices were rising slowly, at, say, 1–2% per year, so you were not very attentive to the small price increases and did not push for any wage rise. The relationship between prices and wages would be weak. But now imagine prices rising at 10% per year. You really would feel the pinch unless your wages were rising by around 10% per year as well. So you ask your boss for a pay rise. You are now much more attentive to changes in the price level. But your wage rise will push up costs, and so prices, which in turn requires you to ask for another and possibly larger pay rise, so wages and prices begin to spiral upwards. Now wages and prices are much more closely related.

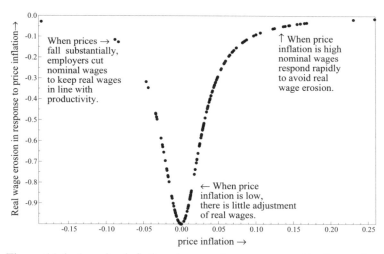

Figure 11.4: As price inflation rises workers are more attentive and act to prevent further erosion of real wages.

This is a form of non-linearity, shown in Figure 11.4. Price inflation plays two roles in determining real wage growth, both directly in eroding real wages and through a 'catch-up' by workers when wages have been eroded by incomplete adjustments to past inflation. Such behavior generates wage-price spirals. The non-linear mapping that captures the evidence is U-shaped; workers become more attentive when price inflation rises, and act to prevent further erosion of their real wages, whereas employers cut nominal wages when prices fall. Figure 11.4 records the shape of this non-linear response, computed from annual data for the UK on prices and wages spanning 1860–2011. When price inflation is small, the failure of wages to react leads to complete erosion, the -1 on the vertical axis: zero inflation induces zero erosion, but that is of course complete. At 5% inflation a 50% erosion is still occurring, and a full offset seems hard for workers to achieve although 90% compensation occurs at 10% inflation.[2]

Another example is that when interest rates are already low, it may prove difficult to stimulate the economy by further reductions. In the aftermath of the Great Recession, interest rates were at a low level in many major economies, and, as interest rates were close to the 'Zero-Lower-Bound', monetary authorities no longer had recourse to their standard policy response. The efficacy of the unconventional monetary policy response to the Crisis by instead adopting Quantitative Easing has been widely debated in the academic literature.[3] From our perspective, this episode illustrates the need to adopt different models in different circumstances.

There are many ways of modeling non-linear responses of one variable to another. A classic example is that an individual's age tends not to have a linear effect on earnings. As age increases beyond a point, the rate at which earnings are expected to increase levels off, and might eventually fall. This can be accommodated in a *linear* relationship where earnings depend on age, and age *squared* (as well as possibly a number of other variables). Here the non-linear response results from including a transformation (the square) of one of the original variables (age) in what is otherwise a linear model. Indeed, that was how Figure 11.4 was generated using a non-linear transformation of price inflation in an otherwise log-linear model of wage inflation.

---

[2] See https://voxeu.org/article/real-wage-productivity-nexus.

[3] See, e.g., Lawrence Summers (2014), 'U.S. Economic Prospects: Secular Stagnation, Hysteresis, and the Zero Lower Bound', *Business Economics* **49**(2).

Switching between several 'regimes'

Returning to our motorist's awful journey, she will have noticed marked differences in her average speed between urban and rural, and between small country roads and motorways. This is an example of switching between 'regimes', here defined by either speed limits or road conditions. Such switches are non-linear in the sense that average speed is not linear in the distance traveled but changes between various bands. Figure 11.5 illustrates for artificial data, where she is traveling quickly along a motorway when the line is near 1 on the vertical axis, then enters a speed-restricted area when it is near 0. The horizontal axis is the distance traveled in each regime. A rather different picture would result from plotting the time spent in each regime, since slow speeds entail much longer times.

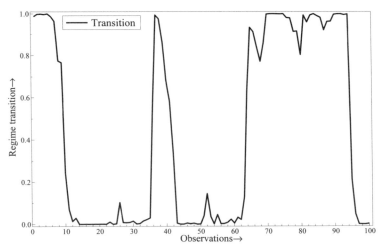

Figure 11.5: Probabilities of being in either the 'fast' regime (close to 1) or the slow regime (which is then shown by closeness to 0).

Similarly, a type of non-linear model often used in time-series applications generally supposes that the model's parameters alter as the value of one or more variables changes. For example, in a two-regime model of the business cycle, there is a regime which explains the evolution of output growth in a recession, and a regime that explains output growth in an expansion. The regime-switching model is predicated on the assumption that the internal dynamics are different between the two regimes. Output growth responds differently to past output growth in expansions and contractions (or to the other variables in the model in the case that the model is more general). That is, contractions, say, are not solely due to a sequence of adverse shock (negative values of the model's random errors): the way that shocks are propagated also depends on the regime. As with the car journey, such a two-regime model specifies which regime the model is in at each point in time, and tries to forecast when it switches between the regimes.

With a sat-nav, our driver will see a town approaching well before she reaches it, so will forecast that a regime switch in her speed is imminent. In economics, suppose the regime operating today will be the recession regime when output growth last period was negative, and otherwise the expansion regime will generate output growth this period. In terms of forecasting from last period, the forecasts will differ depending on whether the economy (according to the model) is in recession or expansion, which would not influence non-switching formulations. In some settings, this can be a useful way of capturing differences in how the economy responds to a large negative shock as opposed to normal times. But unlike the driver's sat-nav, not knowing the route ahead implies that such a model will not be able to forecast recessions, or indeed other switches in regime, ahead of time.

Nevertheless, such non-linear models might be useful for forecasting once the break has occurred, for example, after the transition from normal times to recession. But in general such models are not able to forecast regime-switches well, and still less are they able to forecast breaks. A qualification here is that some regime-switching models may have regimes determined by variables that are 'leading indicators' for recessions. For example, if the regime in operation today depends on an earlier value of some variable, then that regime can be forecast. But this goes back to the requirements for breaks to be predictable. Here, the relevant information is known ahead of time, so it is not the non-linearity of the model per se that permits the regime switch to be forecast. Moreover, if we wished to forecast the regime switch two periods ahead, we would need to have a way of forecasting the value of the variable that triggers the switch, so the forecasting problem has simply been pushed back a stage. Regime-switching models capture regular, recurrent changes between periods of persistent positive growth and typically shorter periods of negative growth (in the business cycle example). Although there are two distinct regimes in operation, the regular switching means that the data are nevertheless stationary. Structural breaks constitute non-stationarities.

In terms of the discussion of black swans, consider the problem of predicting the arrival of the very first black swan. This is the problem of predicting a break. Suppose now that black swans have established regular migratory patterns, so that seasonal sightings are commonplace. Sightings of blacks swans could be modeled by a regime-switching process: because the switching process is seasonal, the regimes are highly predictable in this instance, though perhaps varying, say, with exceptionally warm or cold springs.

As well as the abrupt switching-processes just described, 'smooth transition' models are also popular. As before, there are expansion and recession regimes, but the transition between them is assumed to be gradual. For example, a loss in consumer confidence leading to deficient demand might show up in greater weight being placed on the recession regime. All the models of this sort are estimated on the basis of past business cycle observations, which requires that business cycles are relatively homogeneous episodes, which is not consistent with a pattern of several short recessions and few large and persistent ones.

Numerous other non-linear models have been developed to capture regime shifts. But, despite considerable effort, the empirical evidence on their forecasting performance does not suggest they have been a resounding success. Non-linear models can allow too much flexibility. The model may fit very well in-sample, suggesting the potential to forecast well out-of-sample, but may be capturing accidental features which do not repeat, and hence do not contribute to an improved forecasting performance. The literature also suggests that how well we can predict using a non-linear model relative to a linear model might depend on 'where we are', such that non-linear models outperform during abnormal times, such as when the economy is in recession, as opposed to when the economy is in a steady expansion. So if we were to evaluate the forecasts conditional on the economy being in recession, say, then regime-switching models might be expected to outperform linear models—oh for an economic equivalent of our driver's sat-nav!

The costs of mis-forecasting hurricanes

Tropical cyclones, like hurricanes and typhoons, have long wreaked havoc, as in the 'kamikazes' or divine winds that saved Japan from Mongol invasions in the late 13th Century, but drowned thousands of invading troops.[4]

On September 8, 1900, the 'Galveston Hurricane' hit Galveston, an island close to the coast of Texas south-east of Houston. This hurricane is estimated to have killed around 8,000 people and destroyed more than 3,600 homes, making it the deadliest hurricane and natural disaster in US history. The huge loss of life was due to a combination of the low-lying island of Galveston being swamped by a 15ft storm surge that smashed the city's wooden dwellings, augmented by a failure to forecast the path of the hurricane and the likely ferocity of the storm until too late to evacuate or build viable defenses. Indeed, as the hurricane was about to strike, rail passengers were traveling from Houston to Galveston so suffered a disaster. Never has the cost of hurricane forecast errors been so high.

A massive swirling storm such as in Figure 11.6 evokes awe at its power for potential destruction. Conversely, the ability to take such an amazing photograph emphasizes the possibility of at least forecasting its near-term location, and hence providing advance warning of its approach. Recently, a number of major hurricane-related disasters have hit the USA, including Katrina, Sandy, Harvey, Irma, Florence and Michael. The National Hurricane Center of the National Oceanic and Atmospheric Administration (NOAA) uses a variety of models for the north Atlantic and

---

[4]See Kerry Emanuel, *Divine Wind: The History and Science of Hurricanes*, Oxford University Press, 2005.

Figure 11.6: Typhoon Maysak seen from the International Space Station at 21:18:54 UTC on March 31, 2015: source NASA.

Caribbean areas, including large systems embodying all the known physical relationships, combined with rapidly updated measures of relevant weather variables, to determine the behavior of emerging hurricanes, from which to compute their likely trajectories. Even so, the future path at any time is uncertain, with quite wide interval forecasts as Figure 11.7 shows for Hurricane Irma.[5]

To read the information in the static graphic in Figure 11.7, the small circle on the lower right (denoted 2pm Wed) is the center of the hurricane at the time shown; the dark line with circles shows the most likely trajectory with expected arrival times, whereas their symbol, here **M**, denotes the highest windspeed (i.e., greater than 110 mph). The solid bulb contains the probable path; and the transparent bulb with dots represents the uncertainty around the future track. Alongside, or inside, the solid

---

[5] See its animation at https://www.nhc.noaa.gov/archive/2017/IRMA_graphics.php?product =5day_cone_with_line.

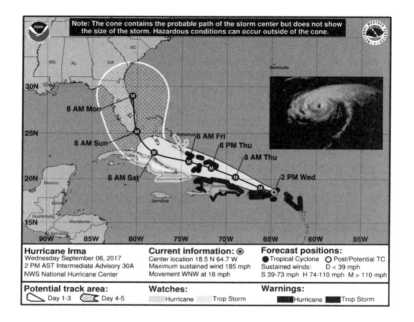

Figure 11.7: Hurricane Irma 2pm Wednesday September 6, 2017, with the magnitude of a typical hurricane (here Floyd) relative to Florida superimposed to illustrate the scale: source NOAA.

bulb, the dark splodges are hurricane warnings usually issued several days ahead, and the lighter ones are watching.

An analysis of Atlantic hurricane damages by Andrew Martinez using *Autometrics* found a significant role was played in the resulting damages by mis-forecasting the landfall of hurricanes (12-hour ahead track error), in addition to the expected physical forces such as maximum wind speed, maximum rainfall, minimum barometric pressure, and maximum storm surge.[6] Damages naturally also depend on the value-at-risk measured by

---

[6]See http://dx.doi.org/10.2139/ssrn.3070154, 2018.

income and the number of housing units. The reason forecast errors matter is they influence the extent of preparation, and even evacuation, facing the onslaught: why prepare if the hurricane will not affect you?

Martinez also documents a great improvement by NOAA in the accuracy of forecasting the paths of hurricanes over the last 60 years (measured by the distance between landfall location and the 12-hour-ahead forecast location produced 12 hours before landfall). Such improvements save lives and reduce physical damages by adaptation, mitigation, and better early warnings. Nevertheless, sudden changes in a hurricane's path—as with Irma veering from a forecast path up the eastern coast of Florida as in Figure 11.7 to actually tracking the western—matter if, say, an evacuation inadvertently takes people into the storm rather than away, or the area that is actually hit had not prepared (e.g., with sandbags and boarding up). Martinez shows that a 1% decrease in the forecast error leads to between 0.25%–0.5% decrease in damages: investing in better forecasts is clearly worthwhile for areas of valuable real estate.[7]

Readers will recognize many of the common elements that affect forecast errors generally. Sudden unanticipated changes (such as location shifts) are pernicious, and rapid adaptation of the forecasts are then needed, but depend on timely observations being incorporated in good models. Perhaps showing the size of the storm (as superimposed on Figure 11.7) with a loose grading of uncertainty away from the central path, as in fan charts, but with just a few bands, as NOAA shows for windspeeds, might clarify the magnitude of the looming problem and the increasing uncertainty over time around the current probable trajectory.

Forecasting climate after a volcanic eruption

Chapter 9 explained indicator saturation to detect outliers and structural breaks. But what if the break exhibited a regular transition path as in Figure 11.1? Then we could combine impulse indicator saturation with the

---

[7] The value of improved hurricane forecasting is considered by Richard Katz and Jeffrey Lazo, 'Economic value of weather and climate forecasts', *Oxford Handbook of Economic Forecasting*, 2011.

'regularized' break path to forecast the transition to a new equilibrium following a break. We call such an exercise 'designer break saturation', and, just as you would expect a designer handbag to be bespoke, the indicators themselves are bespoke to the problem at hand and use subject-matter theory to inform their shape. Let's investigate.

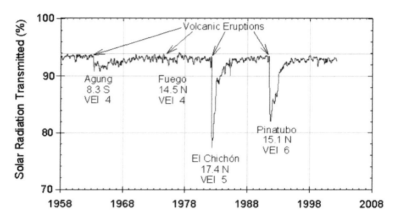

Figure 11.8: Solar radiation transmitted as measured at the Mauna Loa Observatory, 1958–2003, with volcanic eruptions recorded: source NOAA.

Forecasting volcanic eruptions remains difficult, but once they have erupted, they cause the global air temperature to cool due to the sulphate aerosols forced into the atmosphere.[8] Figure 11.8 shows how the solar radiation transmitted has been affected by some relatively recent volcanic eruptions, as measured at the Mauna Loa Observatory. Can we predict how the global air temperature will change after a large volcanic eruption such as El Chichón, or even Pinatubo? Let's use a designed break function to do so.

---

[8] Pretis, Lea Schneider, Jason Smerdon, and Hendry (2016), 'Detecting volcanic eruptions in temperature reconstructions by designed break-indicator saturation', *Journal of Economic Surveys* **30**.

You'll observe in Figure 11.8 that the shape of the response following a volcanic eruption is relatively standard from emissions reducing solar radiation. There is an initial sharp drop in temperature, followed by a gradual return to 'normal'. This pattern can be mapped into a designed break indicator, two possibilities for which are plotted in Figure 11.9.

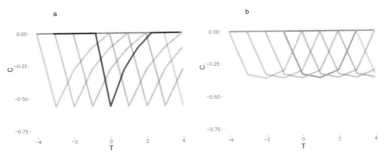

Figure 11.9: (a) 'ν' and (b) 'u' shaped response, plotted for every observation from four periods before to four after a possible eruption date denoted T showing the saturating set over the 8 observations.

The left-hand panel shows a 'ν' shaped response, plotted for every observation starting at 4 observations before a possible eruption, to 4 after, whereas on the right-hand panel we have a more 'u' shaped response. Surface air temperature will drop following a volcanic eruption, but the pace at which it is hypothesized to return to previous levels varies between the two functions.

These break indicators are generated for every observation in the sample and the model is 'saturated' by the designed break indicators as explained for step indicator saturation in Chapter 9. The search procedure throws out most of the indicators as irrelevant, that is, not matching an initial sharp fall in temperature, hence those that are kept correspond most closely to the dates at which volcanoes erupted as measured by a jump in sulphate aerosols—but with no prior knowledge of when these eruptions occurred.

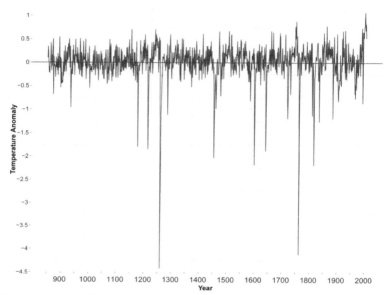

Figure 11.10:   Northern hemisphere model mean surface temperature anomaly relative to 1850–1999: source NCAR.

Figure 11.10 from National Center for Atmospheric Research (NCAR) Coupled and Paleoclimate Model Intercomparison Projects 5 & 3, records the temperature in the northern hemisphere based on dendrochronological temperature reconstructions over the last 1200 years. There are many sudden drops, ranging from 0.5°C to 4.5°C. The exercise we are discussing generated many runs of artificial data simulating Figure 11.10 using small perturbations of the measured sulphate aerosols to create the temperature drop, and for each run the *Autometrics* software sought to locate the eruptions using the ν designer break indicators.

The resulting frequency with which retained break indicators corresponded to the known volcanic eruptions simulated over the period 1550–2005 are recorded in the top half of Figure 11.11, where the corresponding

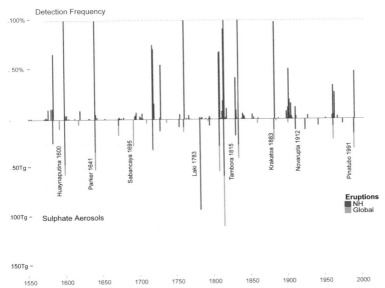

Figure 11.11: Frequency of retaining ν shaped break indicators in simulations for 1550–2005 (NH denotes northern hemisphere).

volumes of sulphate aerosols erupted are shown in the lower half. Large volcanic eruptions are judged by the magnitudes of their sulphate aerosol emissions, and the ν shaped indicators have managed to pick up those erupting 50 teragrams (Tg) or more almost 100% of the time.

So the big question is: can we use this model to forecast the temperature recovery? The break has to be in train—we are not forecasting the volcanic eruption, but the temperature in the years immediately after the eruption. We require that the break function we choose is well specified and that we have a method to capture the break evolution. In practice, the choice of break function would be made on the basis of observed breaks, so we require that the future form of the break resembles the past occurrences.

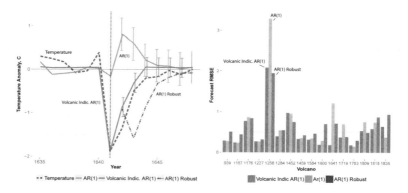

Figure 11.12: Left panel—'forecasting' the temperature recovery after the eruption of Parker, 1641; right panel—root mean square forecast errors for 16 major eruptions.

To illustrate, we consider the 1641 volcanic eruption of Parker in the Philippines. The forecast origin is set to the year of the eruption, so that the forecast-origin observation captures the immediate (within-year) temperature drop, which determines the depth of the 'ν' (solid line). The eruption trajectory is also 'forecast' (albeit retrospectively) with various other forecasting devices. The designer break function (thick dashed line with bars) tracks the actual temperature movements relatively closely, unlike the simple model using just one past observation of the data to explain the current outcome (called an autoregressive model and denoted AR(1), solid line with bars) that is not able to model the break. The autoregressive model forecasts rise instead of falling. This is because it is an 'equilibrium correction' model, and as such, its forecasts revert to the model's mean.

The robust adjustment to the autoregressive model (AR(1) Robust, and shown as a dotted line) also performs rather poorly, emphasizing the advantages of designing break indicators relevant to the situation under analysis. Here the initial fall is not a location shift, and the recovery has commenced before the differencing takes effect, so its forecasts of the fall are too late and hence in the wrong direction. The average of the forecasts from the autoregressive model and its differenced version would have performed substantially better than either alone, but still worse than the designed indicator.

The right-hand panel reports the RMSFEs for the three devices for sixteen salient historical volcanic eruptions.[9] The designed indicator approach produces noticeably worse forecasts only for the 1835 eruption of Cosigüina, Nicaragua. Conversely, the designed indicator approach substantially outperforms for the massive 1257–58 eruption of Samalas in Indonesia which led to a well-documented famine in Europe, as did its neighbor Tambora in 1815, which caused the 'year without a summer' in 1816, when snow fell in June in Massachusetts, as well as inspiring J.M.W. Turner's colorful paintings of sunsets, and the writing by Mary Wollstonecraft Shelley of *Frankenstein, or the Modern Prometheus.*

As mentioned earlier, the flexibility afforded by a non-linear model can be a double-edged sword. Non-linear models typically fit the data better within sample than simpler linear models, but the improved fit need not translate into a superior out-of-sample forecast performance. A structured approach, such as designer break saturation, has the potential to do well, as shown above, once the break has occurred, at least assuming the designer-break shape is correct and that future shifts resemble past shifts.

---

[9]From Schneider, Smerdon, Pretis, Claudia Hartl-Meier and Jan Esper (2017): http://iopscience.iop.org/article/10.1088/1748-9326/aa7a1b/meta.

Chapter 12

Would more information be useful?

Oddly, the industry that is the primary engine of this incredible pace of change—the computer industry—turns out to be rather bad at predicting the future itself. There are two things in particular that it failed to see: one was the coming of the Internet; the other was the end of the century.
Douglas Adams, *The Salmon of Doubt*, Basingstoke: Macmillan, 2002.

Would more information help our motorist more accurately forecast her journey time? If it were the right information, then it would help by definition, because that is what we mean by 'right' in this context. In fact, the term 'information' can mean a number of different things. Often we mean by information the numerical data observations on which forecasts are based. For example, that might be the past history of values of the variable we wish to forecast, if we want to calculate the mean value to forecast with, or, better still, an estimate of the mean adjusted for shifts and outliers. However, 'information' can be used in a wider sense to refer to knowing the distributions of the variables to be forecast (i.e., Normal or not); whether variables react immediately or with a delay; which explanatory variables matter for the variable to be forecast and which are irrelevant; and also to knowing how they are related (e.g., linearly or not, with constant parameters etc.). This last form of information could include the elusive aspect of what determines location shifts.

In the economics sphere, at least, the information age is in full swing and a vast amount of information is available, from the latest releases of economics statistics; to surveys of expectations, opinions, and confidence about the prospects for the economy; to the 'prices' determined by the operation of prediction markets; to 'big data' generated by text in the form of news stories and commentaries, and social media activities. Determining what constitutes the 'right information' would appear to be a herculean task. Before we tackle this, let's consider again the more mundane everyday task of journeying from A to B.

Suppose our motorist wishes to make a trip. She has at her disposal hour-by-hour data on the rate of traffic flow on all the roads in the areas she wishes to pass through, for yesterday and for the previous nine days. She might assume that today will be similar to recent days, and make use of all the hourly data on all the potential roads she might travel on to determine the route with the shortest journey time, and this would then determine her forecast. Or she might have a preferred route, perhaps involving a scenic journey, or one that avoids toll roads, and just wants to calculate how long that journey will take. She might use yesterday's data on average speeds for the different sections of her journey, or she might consider the conditions over the previous ten days. Or simply use the fact that it's a Friday, and traffic is always heavier on a Friday, and so add ten minutes to her 'best guess'.

Is there any benefit to using the hourly data on traffic flow on the different sections of her route, either from yesterday or from (any of) the previous days? Possibly, but improvements in the accuracy of her forecast could be offset by not accounting for other information, such as systematic day-to-day variation (such as the heavier traffic on a Friday) or the weather, and so on. More information would help if the day-to-day variation can be modeled alongside the hour-of-the-day variation in road congestion, and all other factors, but otherwise any improvements might be disappointing.

So the answer to the question posed in the chapter title is, 'It depends'. Adding more information need not avert a forecast failure, unless the information in question alerts the motorist or economic forecaster to the coming shift: we consider this possibility again below, but have already noted that a sat-nav warning of a jam may enable her to divert and avoid the congestion.

In economics it might be difficult to determine which of the large set of potentially relevant variables to include in the model. The motorist's task is simpler in that we know that the factors determining travel time are average speed and distance. Speed is in turn determined by congestion, and congestion is determined by the number of drivers who are in their cars on that stretch of road at that time relative to its capacity. Forecasting that number might be difficult as it depends on the decisions of all the individuals who chose to undertake a car journey that puts them on that stretch of road at that time (and of course all those who chose not to!), although in aggregate the number may not vary much between weekdays (given the time of the day) as humans are creatures of habit. Nevertheless, at least in principle we know what it is we need to know. In macroeconomics there is often disagreement about the key determinants of variables of interest, or at least about the relative importance of the determining factors. Take inflation as an example: is inflation mainly caused by the growth rate of the money supply, or the excess of demand over supply for goods and services (and/or labor), or the prices of imported goods, or expectations of inflation (which affect wage negotiations), and so on?

If there are a number of candidate determinants (or explanatory variables), the past data might be informative about which variables best explained the variable of interest over the historical period. If the number of potential determinants is large, and the historical record is relatively short, precisely determining the effects of the various putative explanatory variables might not be possible. Although the Bank of England website boasts a spreadsheet containing 'A millennium of macroeconomic data', which suggests the length of the historical record would appear to be ample even for a large number of potential explanatory variables, the problem is that relationships between variables that held at the time of the Domesday Book are not necessarily a good guide to the workings of the modern day economy.[1] Thus, forecasters sometimes 'pool' the available information to produce a smaller set of potential determinants, and may also pool or combine forecasts from different models. We consider these in turn.

Pooling information

One popular way of proceeding is to take a large set of variables, which might consist of quarterly observations over 20 or 30 years for 100 or more variables, and calculate a small number of 'principal components' (also called 'factors'), usually between one and five, intended to capture the key movements. The data must have an appropriate 'structure' for this step to be successful. There have to be common movements across the variables, so that most of the variation in each of the original 100 or more variables can be captured by the much smaller number of factors. Think of this occurring because each of the variables is a linear combination of all the factors. Then, by choosing the weight allocated to every variable, one can form combinations of the variables that reflect the underlying 'factors'. It does seem possible in practice to reduce the dimension of large datasets of economic variables in this way. In recent years, factor models have been used as one way of dealing with the high dimensionality of the potential set of relevant variables. The small number of factors can then be included in the forecasting model of the variable of interest instead of many separate explanatory variables. However, the results on whether including 'more information' this way is helpful, namely in terms of adding factors to simple dynamic models, are somewhat mixed.

Are simple models best?

What is the reason for the equivocal findings concerning the forecasting performance of models which make use of such large amounts of information? One of the key problems seems to be the need to forecast the future

---

[1] http://www.bankofengland.co.uk/research/Pages/datasets/default.aspx#threecenturies.

values of the factors in order to generate the forecasts of the variable of interest, say inflation. That is, inflation is contemporaneously related to the factors, whereas for forecasting, we need the factors to lead inflation. Then we can use the current values of the factors known today to forecast future movements in inflation. All models which incorporate a contemporaneous response of the target variable to the explanatory variables have this drawback, which is the more acute the more difficult it is to accurately forecast the future values of the explanatory variables. The other key problem is that location shifts will still precipitate forecast failure unless an adaptive formulation is adopted.

Indeed, the finding from 'forecasting competitions'—where many hundreds of different variables are forecast over many periods of time by dozens of approaches—is that simple models do better than more complicated ones in terms of various measures of forecast accuracy.[2] However, we showed above that robust forecasting devices can avoid systematic forecast failure after location shifts, and many simple models happen to be robust, so that characteristic may explain the outcomes of 'forecasting competitions', rather than simplicity. A large model based on a great deal of information, possibly including factors, could do well in such competitions if modified to a robust representation, whereas the simplest model of the sample mean will often perform badly.

Pooling forecasts

When you have different forecasts of the same phenomenon, let's say the Greenbook forecasts and the OECD forecasts of US economic growth over the next year, which one should you use? Unless you have evidence that one is clearly superior, why not use both? A combination, where forecasts are combined from different models to produce a single forecast, can often be better than a single forecast alone. Forecast combination has a long history and is very common, suggesting that there is value in combining forecasts. But why not just select the 'best' forecast and stick with it? Think

---

[2] The most recent M4 competition involved forecasting 100,000 variables at a number of frequencies over a variety of horizons: https://www.mcompetitions.unic.ac.cy/.

of forecast combination as an insurance policy. You aren't sure which is the best forecast, so the pooling of forecasts from different approaches or models can lead to canceling offsetting biases. When models use different information sets, or are differentially susceptible to structural breaks, then combination can be advantageous. As we noted for the left-hand panel in Figure 11.12, an average of the forecasts from the autoregressive model and its robust version would outperform either alone.

If the past was a good guide to the future, then you could look at the historical forecast performance record to see if the informational content of one model dominates all others, called forecast encompassing. If so, the other forecasting models are redundant and the preferred model forecast encompasses them. If not, so comparisons between forecasts do not reveal a single 'winner', then pooling forecasts may provide a better alternative, and of course one can test if the pooled forecast encompasses all the individual ones. This approach is appealing as we can learn more about the underlying process by refining forecasting models and incorporating the superior features of rival forecasting models to improve the 'best' model, a value-adding approach.

Unfortunately the past is not a good guide to the future. The world is constantly changing, and good forecasting models yesterday need not be the best forecasting models today. Forecast encompassing does not negate the benefits of forecast averaging. Furthermore, if we think of the pooling of forecasts as a 'portfolio diversification strategy', pooling can reduce the uncertainty of the forecast.[3]

However, a word of caution. Line up 10 glasses of water. Perhaps add a different flavor cordial to each to represent different forecasting models. Now mix the glasses together. Who knows if it tastes better or worse as a combination. But what if one of those glasses contained a poison? After mixing the drinks together, it would be wise to steer clear of consuming any of the beverages. The moral: when combining forecasting models, any 'poisonous' models that could contaminate the average should be selected out, so model selection is not otiose even when pooling forecasts is

---

[3] Such an interpretation is proposed by Allan Timmermann in the *Handbook of Economic Forecasting*, 2006.

deemed the desired strategy.[4] Forecast combination exercises sometimes recognize this fact and 'trim' the set of candidate forecasts to drop the most extreme.

Using other information

We can readily check whether additional information would have been valuable in any given instance, at least from an historical perspective. We can construct forecasting models using various sets of explanatory variables, and generate forecasts from these models as if they had been made in 'real time', that is, only using data that would have been available to forecasters at each point in the past. Then we can determine how well a particular model, forecasting method, or technique would have fared had it been used historically to generate forecasts for periods for which we now have actual values. This allows us to determine the usefulness of that information set when used for forecasting.

Whether additional information would have resulted in superior forecasts can then be determined by repeating the exercise using the extended information set. If we re-compute the real-time forecasts using a model based on the larger set of information, we can gauge whether more information is better.

A powerful way of considering the value of more information (relative to that contained in a simple forecasting model, such as a univariate device, or a method such as a no-change forecast) is to consider survey expectations. Survey respondents may make use of models, but will typically exercise judgement to incorporate an allowance for information from a potentially wide range of sources. Perhaps not surprisingly, survey forecasts do appear to outperform (various) model forecasts, especially for nominal variables such as inflation. An interesting question is whether this is just because the survey forecasts have superior knowledge of the current state of the economy, and so are better at nowcasting, since getting the 'starting-point' right also gives them an edge over purely model-based forecasts for longer horizons.

---

[4]See http://voxeu.org/article/how-should-we-make-economic-forecasts.

Should we use big or small forecasting models?

The selection of models used for the purpose of forecasting is a topic on which there is little consensus. Parsimony is often cited as an essential aspect of a model's good forecast performance, but large information sets such as those utilized in factor forecasting described above are also seen as driving successful forecasts. The enthusiasm for 'big data' suggests increasing information sets could be a useful tool for forecasting. Conversely, lack of parsimony is often given as a reason for poor forecast performance, with naive devices frequently outperforming either theory-based or data-based forecasting models. There have been many attempts to reconcile this trade-off. So what principles can we take from this literature?

First, more information unambiguously should not worsen predictability. Although this sounds like a clear argument for always using larger datasets, this unfortunately does not map to a statement that more information always improves forecasting. Predictability is necessary but not sufficient for forecastability: there are many steps between the two. The information available may be measured with error, it could enter linearly or non-linearly in the model of the data, the relationships between the information and the phenomena to forecast need to be estimated but could change over time, and forecasts many periods in the future have to rely only on information available today. Given these complications, there are no rules as to the 'optimal' model size for forecasting: the folklore that overfitting (i.e. including too many variables) or a lack of parsimony per se are detrimental for forecasting may be misleading.

A second notable result for forecasters choosing forecasting models is that, for stationary data, variables should be kept in forecasting models at a much looser significance level than conventional critical values would imply. While this sounds rather technical, the implication is that larger models than are typically used ought to be preferable. This result entails that conditioning information should be retained in a forecasting model if it contributes even a small amount to explaining the variable to be forecast. The conventional wisdom in economics is to use, say, a 5% significance level, which implies that there is a 95% chance that the chosen variable is relevant. One forecasting result suggests that variables should be kept if there is roughly an 84% chance that the conditioning information explains, or partly explains, the variable to be forecast, so more conditioning information should be included in the forecasting model.

Third, and again for stationary data, less information should not induce predictive failure. If the forecaster has omitted some variables from their model, then the cost is that the forecasts are likely to have larger uncertainty bands, but that will not lead to forecast failure. This sounds like a great insurance policy. Even if the forecaster selects the wrong model and leaves out an explanatory variable that is relevant, and so would partly explain the variable to be forecast if added to the model, then the costs are not too severe. So, in contrast to the previous two arguments, parsimony need not be too expensive. Smaller models need not lead to forecast failure, so omission may not cost much, at least for stationary data.

Fourth, smaller models could exclude irrelevant information that might shift and therefore cause forecast failure if adventitiously retained. If variables are retained in a model but actually do not explain the variable to be forecast, then movements in these irrelevant variables will erroneously predict changes in the variable to be forecast. Big shifts may cause forecast failure, even if the variable to be forecast has nothing to do with the shifted variable. But the converse is crucial: omitting relevant variables that shift will also cause forecast failure. Government officials may hate economists saying 'on the one hand,. . ., but on the other' and desire one-handed advisers, but, unfortunately, the nature of the real world is unknown, and whether or not a variable that might shift should, or should not, be included in a model can be moot as its 'true' relevance is always uncertain.

Finally, 'causal' models need not outperform naive 'robust' devices in forecasting, even though the 'causal' models are better models in-sample. By 'causal' we mean that the variables in a model really do determine the variable to be forecast. A causal model can be derived from theoretical analysis or by data-based methods, but entails that the forecasting model contains genuinely 'relevant' variables. For example, forecasts of consumption may come from a 'causal' model conditioning on income and inflation and may explain movements in consumption in-sample extremely well. Nevertheless, the forecasts from a random walk model of consumption, where the next prediction of the annual change in consumption is last period's annual change in consumption, can provide more accurate forecasts.[5] Even though the causal model really does explain consumers' expenditure, and the 'robust' model does not, the latter could produce better forecasts. Thus, although your in-sample model may be fantastic, causally based and explain every nuance of the data, it's forecasts need not be superior. As such, good in-sample models are no guide to good forecasting models.

Where does this leave us? Any useful forecasting model needs to be able to reconcile the conflicts of the above theorems.

If only we could forecast shifts!

What form available information takes is crucial. Knowledge that a shift will occur could help forecasts dramatically, and has been a recurrent theme in this book. We have noted examples that occur in every day life, as when a car mechanic correctly recommends new brakes and an accident is avoided several days later. Or when a sat-nav warns to detour to avoid a prolonged delay. Or when a volcanologist alerts those living near a volcano that an eruption seems imminent.[6]

As yet, progress in forecasting economic shifts is minimal, but that is primarily because research on that topic is also minimal and deserves to be greatly increased. Shifts have causes and hence are not inherently unpredictable, so analyses of past major shifts to ascertain possible leading indicators thereof merit study.

There is also a communications issue. When agencies try to foresee problems, as with forecasting the economic consequences of Brexit, they are all too often treated as either fake news or political maneuvres, and quickly misrepresented as wrong when the event on which the forecasts

---

[5]For example, James Davidson and Hendry (1981), 'Interpreting econometric evidence: The behaviour of consumers' expenditure in the UK', *European Economic Review*, **16**.

[6]See https://theconversation.com/were-volcano-scientists-here-are-six-volcanoes-well-be-watching-out-for-in-2018-89051.

are predicated (here actually leaving the EU) has not yet happened. In essence, shifts have political as well as economic implications, so there may be groups with such interests who want to treat the forecasts as not well based.

Despite such manifest difficulties, we have progressed in both understanding how to adapt forecasts rapidly after breaks, as well as forecasting during breaks, so the next stage is to investigate potential 'early warning systems' of impending shifts—reminding us of Robert Fitzroy's earlier efforts.

Chapter 13

Can econometrics improve forecasting?

> Statistician: A man who believes figures don't lie, but admits
> that under analysis some of them won't stand up either.
> Evan Esar, *Esar's Comic Dictionary*, New York: Harvest House
> Publishers, 1943.

Models versus extrapolation (or rules-of-thumb)

Imagine that our motorist is adept at the use of spreadsheet modeling and
decides to build a formal model to forecast her journey times. She thinks
this might yield more accurate forecasts than the less structured approach
she has used to date: she has relied on a combination of the traffic news
and her sat-nav, and on occasion used simple 'rules-of-thumb', such as
assuming the journey will take her as long as a recent journey she has
undertaken of comparable distance.

Her new model is structural in the sense that she attempts to isolate
and include those factors which directly determine journey time. Thus,
she inputs a formula to explain journey time based on the simple physical

law that time taken equals the distance to be traveled in miles (or kilo-meters) divided by average speed, but remember to measure all influences in consistent units—unlike a recent attempted Mars lander! Hence, twice the distance will take twice the time—all else equal (the economists' infamous *ceteris paribus*). She models her journey time for each stage of her journey using this formula, by using as input variables the average speed and distance to be traveled, on the different road types: motorway, dual carriageway, or single lane (but split between high and low quality roads). Each road type has a maximum speed limit, which will affect the average speed likely to be achievable on that stretch. Next, assuming she has a choice of car at her disposal, the type of car, perhaps in three categories (sports, family, rather old), again measured by an estimate of their likely average speeds (*ceteris paribus*), as well as an allowance for her natural caution—or derring-do! Then come various weather and 'calendar effects': time of year, day of the week, time of day when starting, whether a holiday is starting or ending (which may interact with the journey starting time), and so on.

There are many specification decisions to be made, some of which could have a substantive effect on the forecast accuracy of her model. Some relevant factors may be omitted, perhaps through oversight, such as moderating the speed projections using real-time information on traffic congestion, and bad weather, etc. It is likely the spreadsheet model will not be complete and correct, even before unanticipated events intervene (such as unforeseen deviations, closed roads, and so on). Notwithstanding any deficiencies in her model, it is clear that the approach of constructing a structural model to forecast journey time is very different from using a 'rule-of-thumb', such as just assuming the journey time will be equal to that of a 'similar' journey recently undertaken. Although omitting important factors such as congestion may seriously curtail the usefulness of her model as a forecasting device, such models might still be relevant to road planners and highways agencies interested in the likely savings in travel time precisely by improving sections of roads, or building new trunk roads, and so on. Rules-of-thumb will not help in such settings. This comparison is reminiscent of our bus-stop game not helping to forecast volcanic eruptions, whereas a causal model based on appropriate information might.

Nevertheless, rules-of-thumb have a long pedigree in economics, dating back at least to the 1930s in the USA.[1]

To what extent does this example of 'model building' mimic the problems faced by economists as macro-forecasters and as policy advisers? Structural models of the economy are also unlikely to include all the causal channels and influences on the variable or variables being modeled. Indeed, the task facing the economist would appear to be an order of magnitude more difficult, at least in terms of attempting to include in the model all the potential causal factors and influences, given the number and variety of agents whose beliefs, actions and interactions culminate in the observed macroeconomic outcomes. More than 70 years ago, Tjalling Koopmans argued that:

> In dynamic economics, the phenomenon itself is either essentially a stochastic process or needs to be treated as such because of the great number of factors at work.

and suggested that:

> the analysis of each structural equation be pushed to the point where the joint effect of unanalyzed factors can indeed be regarded as random (if not necessarily independent) drawings from a reasonably stable probability distribution.
> Koopmans (1947), 'Measurement without theory', *Review of Economics and Statistics*, **29**.

Koopmans seems to consider it possible to produce economic models that can effectively be regarded as 'closed', in the sense that any remaining omitted causal factors can be treated as random disturbances. If this were the case, then such models could be used for policy analysis and forecasting. An alternative view is that an economic model will at best capture

---

[1] Gabriel Mathy and Herman Stekler (2017), 'Expectations and forecasting during the Great Depression: Real-time evidence from the business press', *Journal of Macroeconomics*, **53**, discuss various rules-of-thumb that were commonly used for forecasting in the USA during the Great Depression of the 1930s, many of which were based on how the economy had performed in earlier recessions: see, e.g., Lewis Haney, *Business Forecasting*, Ginn and Company, 1931.

some causal factors and influences, but will be 'open' in that there are neglected causal influences which exert a systematic influence and cannot be reduced to a random error term. That interpretation suggests such a model could lend itself to policy analysis provided the omitted influences were largely independent of the policy under consideration, but would not be useful for forecasting, as outcomes would be driven in part by factors not included in the model.

We view the 'lack of closure' of structural models as inevitable and intrinsic in economics, as empirical models often seem to suffer from sudden unanticipated shifts in their equilibrium means. These call into question the blind use of such models for forecasting, while accepting they may have some potential for policy analysis when a forecast failure does not impugn the planned intervention.

All models are not born equal

The previous discussion bears on an evaluation of theory-based versus data-based models in economics both for forecasting and policy analysis. Many economists seem to believe 'those that can, do theory; and those that cannot, forecast', and treat forecast failures as showing the ineptitude of the latter. However, recent research has revealed that the central mathematical tools used in modern macroeconomic theory based on intertemporal optimizing behavior of economic agents necessarily assume that distributions of outcomes do not shift unexpectedly between time periods. When they do, the assumption that economic agents know what will happen on average in future periods is violated. Consequently, and unlike our Apollo mission example, to every macroeconomic forecast failure due to an unexpected location shift there is an accompanying theory failure.

This problem was already present in Figure 2.2, a variant of which we now consider. Imagine an office worker planning her spending for next period on the assumption that there will be no change in her income, denoted 'Originally expected average outcome' in Figure 13.1. Unfortunately, the company she works for suddenly announces bankruptcy and her income falls sharply, denoted 'Unexpected shift in the mean' on the figure. Clearly her plan is greatly disrupted: but a theory that does not allow for such shifts assumes that she will continue to act as before.

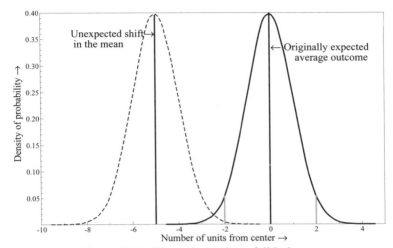

Figure 13.1: Illustrating a sharp fall in income.

Indeed, 'rational' economic theories often entail that it would be irrational for her not to assume that the future looks like the past, and hence she should expect the same average outcome tomorrow as she experienced today. Worse still, such theory, which determines the dominant model form at many of the world's central banks, imposes the 'Originally expected average outcome' as the equilibrium and hence will converge back to it irrespective of where the data actually go. Consequently, such models will suffer systematic forecast failure after a location shift—till either that model is abandoned or a robust version adopted, which is essentially replacing a theory-based approach by a data-based one. Such models have the grand title of 'dynamic stochastic general equilibrium' (DSGE) systems, and their assumption about how the economy's participants form expectations for the future is called 'rational expectations', despite it being obvious from Figure 13.1 that it would be completely irrational to

always assume tomorrow will be like today in a world where shifts occur. And, yes, DSGEs treat the economy as having a single 'representative
agent'—whom we can call Robinson Crusoe—who is assumed to behave
according to a very abstract version of economic theory. Inequality cannot
exist, and why Robinson keeps his own wages low to maximize his profits,
then tries to avoid paying taxes to himself is unclear.

As an illustrative case, the Bank of England ditched its 'old-fashioned'
empirical models in favor of a DSGE model, known as the Bank of England Quarterly Model (BEQM, pronounced Beckham), a complex model
that took several years and significant person-power to develop.[2] One
might hope that a model based on the most up-to-date macroeconomic theory from some of the brightest minds using the best available data would
yield successful forecasts, but all did not augur well for BEQM—the financial crisis led to its breakdown. In August 2008 the model predicted
'the central projection was for GDP to be broadly flat for the next year or
so': the eagle-eyed amongst you will observe that this is when the Great
Recession began. Criticisms of BEQM then abounded, with many other
economists quick to point out that, in addition to its many flawed assumptions, the model did not have a role for credit or liquidity, effectively leaving it impotent to understanding, explaining or forecasting the Financial
Crisis.

How did the Bank of England respond to the failure of its central
model? In 2011 it built a new economic model, but based on exactly the
same DSGE principles as the previously discredited system, despite the
flaws in the mathematics used for its derivation. This model, known as
COMPASS, for the Central Organizing Model for Projection Analysis and
Scenario Simulation, was a slimmed down version of the previous BEQM
model, intended to be easier to operate. In order to plug the holes in the
smaller model, where COMPASS was silent on some aspects of the economy, it was accompanied by a suite of other models to provide forecasts
for 'missing channels'. Known collectively as CAST (COMPASS and
Suite Transition), the core DSGE model and supporting suite of ad hoc

---

[2]The model is decribed in *The Bank of England Quarterly Model*, London: Bank of
England, 2005.

models are key inputs to the Monetary Policy Committee (MPC), providing the framework for the Bank of England's published macroeconomic forecasts.

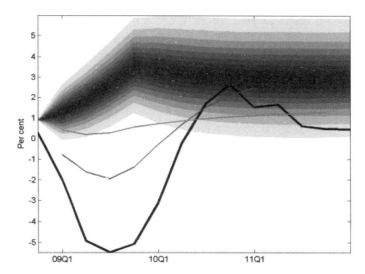

Figure 13.2: Annual GDP growth forecasts from 2008:Q4. Annual output growth ('first final' equivalent) in the thick line, COMPASS density forecast as a shaded fan, Statistical Suite forecasts are closest to that, with the *Inflation Report* forecasts in the thinner line closest to the outcomes.

So how would this new DSGE model have fared over the Great Recession? Disastrously! The model-based 'forecasts', computed after the event, exhibited systematic forecast failure, as can be seen in Figure 13.2.[3] This graph, from the Bank of England, shows the model-based forecasts

---

[3]The figure is our replication of Figure 1(b) in Nicholas Fawcett, Riccardo Masolo, Lena Körber, and Matt Waldron, https://bankunderground.co.uk/2015/11/20/how-did-the-banks-forecasts-perform-before-during-and-after-the-crisis/.

for annual GDP growth from COMPASS as the fan forecasts, with the outturns in the thick black line. The COMPASS forecasts add a survey measure of one-year ahead growth expectations to the set of observables, which leads to an improvement in GDP growth forecasts.[4] 'State of the art' economic theory and best practice by the Bank's economic forecasters would have been unable to prevent the recurrence of forecast failure on a grand scale from their new model. 'Learn from past mistakes' should be part of everyone's motto.

The thin line that is initially closest to the outcomes records the forecasts from the Bank of England's *Inflation Report*. This is the MPC's best collective judgement about the most likely paths for inflation and output, so they contain judgemental information. The other thin line, initially closest to the fans, records the forecasts from the statistical suite of models, CAST, so differs from the distribution forecasts of COMPASS in that the forecasting models are not based purely on underlying economic theory, but are also trying to capture empirical regularities. All the forecasts condition on information that was available in real time, but the *Inflation Report* forecasts are able to include timely data such as survey indicators and expert judgement which improved the accuracy of the short-term forecasts relative to the model-based forecasts of COMPASS.[5]

Again we see the problem with using equilibrium-correction models for forecasting after a location shift: COMPASS forecasts a rise in GDP growth when the data fall sharply. Figure 13.2 also shows that the longer-term forecasts come back on track as the recession flattens off—the data again moving to the model not vice versa. While such difficulties are common to all equilibrium-based forecasting systems as noted above, DSGEs emphasize that they are 'general equilibrium' formulations, so do not include any mechanisms for Robinson to correct his mistakes. Certainly few people, expert or not, forecast the timing and magnitude of the Financial Crisis: the resulting location shift caused forecast failure in most models, and also nowcast failures by statistics agencies. Nevertheless, there is less

---

[4] See Fawcett *et al.* (2015) for details.

[5] If the COMPASS forecasts are conditioned on the one and two quarter ahead Staff Short Term Inflation Forecasts, then they are more in line with the *Inflation Report* forecasts: see Fawcett *et al.* (2015) for details.

of an excuse for failure to rapidly adapt forecasts after the Crisis and to repeat a failed modeling approach.

As discussed in Chapter 7, although DSGE models such as BEQM had no financial sector, that was probably not why they missed forecasting the financial crisis or suffered forecast failure from that omission. The theory-model versus statistical-model distinction is relevant across a range of disciplines.[6] However, macroeconomic theory is not a unique entity, and need not make the many strong assumptions explicit in DSGEs. The Crisis should have acted as a catalyst for a major rethink of macroeconomics, not raised the drawbridge to protect the previous approach.[7]

Are 'good' forecasting models useful for policy?

As we have seen from earlier chapters, economies shift about all the time, with unanticipated shocks prevalent. Change is the norm. But some changes matter more than others. Take a look at the three panels of Figure 13.3. Let's play a game of spot the difference.

At observation 41 on the horizontal axis, the model that generated the data shifted. In fact, every parameter in the model shifted, so the model is unrecognizable compared to the model that generated the data prior to observation 41. You can easily observe the U-shaped trajectory common in recessions. But what we haven't told you, and what the policy maker would not know, is that in each of the three panels all the links between the variables have changed in very different ways. For example, some of the parameters are doubled, some are halved, and others are changed by even larger amounts. This poses a problem for the policy maker. We can see that there has been a shift, but we have no idea what the new model is. If we correctly guessed the coefficients that led to the trajectory in Panel

---

[6] See the discussion by Graham Hatch, 'Modelling and forecasting at the Bank of England' in *Understanding Economic Forecasts*, and several of the chapters in Part IV of *Oxford Handbook of Economic Forecasting*.

[7] See http://voxeu.org/article/improved-approach-empirical-modelling-0, and Hendry and John Muellbauer (2018), 'The future of macroeconomics: Macro theory and models at the Bank of England', *Oxford Review of Economic Policy*, **34**.

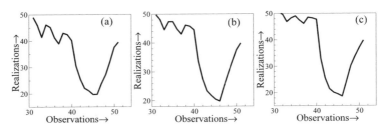

Figure 13.3: Many parameters can shift. A break is replicated by changing different combinations of parameters: economic agents could not tell what had shifted till long afterwards.

(a) and based policy (such as an interest rate decision) on this, all would be well. But if the 'correct' shifted parameters were those in Panels (b) or (c), we could be implementing the wrong policy.

So how can we generate data that look so similar but be based on very different parameterizations? The key is the effect on the equilibrium. All three panels have an equilibrium that shifts from 50 to approximately 20 in observation 41 and back to 50 again at observation 46. This equilibrium is determined by a combination of all the model parameters. Any of the parameters can shift but essentially their only observable effect is on the mean of the process. It will take many periods after the shift to detect individual parameter changes, far too late for forecasting and policy to be effective. How do we interpret this difficulty? In Chapter 7, we argued that unanticipated shifts in long-run means were likely to cause forecast failure, and that such shifts would be readily apparent with hindsight.

But what if other changes in parameters were not easily detectable? Indeed, the converse case is where the changes to the parameters affecting the equilibrium neatly cancel. From Chapter 7, $(a+bc)$ could stay constant when all three parameters shifted if in fact $a = d - bc$ for a fixed value of d. Then, like the above graphs, however much a, b, c shifted, a similar outcome would be observed. Changes in how rapidly the economy adjusts to a shock can take some time to be noticed. Hooray for forecasting—if changes are not noticeable, they are unlikely to pose a problem for forecasting. But beware: any policy based on the wrong model will usually be wrong. So, although shifts that are not easily detectable are less of a concern for forecasting, they are not innocuous for policy. The timing of the effects of policy changes are most susceptible to this problem.

From forecasting to forediction

Forecasts are used to make policy decisions by many agencies, so the two are often closely interconnected. The term 'forediction' was coined by Hendry in 2001 as a neologism to replace 'forecasting', because his new term had not yet acquired the many negative connotations attached to words of greater antiquity as noted in Chapter 2. Forediction captures the notion of a close link between a forecast and an accompanying narrative, so is intended here to convey a *fore*cast made alongside a story (*diction*) describing that forecast verbally, and often also used to justify a policy decision claimed to be entailed by the forecast. As an example, in their 'Macroeconomic forecasting: debunking a few old wives' tales', Discussion paper 395, Research Department, Banca d'Italia (2001), Stefano Siviero and Daniele Terlizzese state that:

> forecasting does not simply amount to producing a set of figures: rather, it aims at assembling a fully-fledged view—one may call it a 'story behind the figures'—of what could happen: a story that has to be internally consistent, whose logical plausibility can be assessed, whose structure is sufficiently articulated to allow one to make a systematic comparison with the wealth of information that accumulates as time goes by.

Central banks typically produce numerical forecasts of key economic variables: think of the Bank of England's inflation forecasts (known as rivers of blood because their fan charts appear in red) and GDP forecasts (rivers of bile). Accompanying these numerical forecasts are textual explanations of the forecasts, given, for example, in *Inflation Reports*. Policy decisions, such as a rise in the interest rate, would be based on both the numerical forecast and textual explanation, that is, the forediction. Indeed, the text is often sufficiently close to the published forecast that a 'derived' forecast can be obtained (using textual analysis) that is in turn very close to the direct numerical forecast. If the numerical forecast turns out to exhibit forecast failure, then so will the derived forecast, which refutes the underlying narrative and hence results in forediction failure. That in turn implies policy invalidity. This provides a direct link between forecast performance and policy decisions. Further, it is a testable link, so foredictions and associated policy decisions can be explicitly evaluated, but only after the event when the numerical forecast can be evaluated relative to the outcome, by which time the policy would have been implemented.

There are four steps to evaluating foredictions and resulting policy decisions. First, the numerical forecasts must be closely described by the accompanying narrative. If the story can be quantified in derived forecasts, these should closely match the original numerical forecasts. Second, test the numerical, and hence derived, forecasts for evidence of forecast failure. If those forecasts are reasonably accurate given their uncertainty bands, and the narrative matches the numerical forecasts, then policy based on that narrative is sensible. But if there is forecast failure of the numerical forecasts, then the narrative must be rejected.

Third, if a policy implementation is justified by the forediction, then forediction failure will invalidate the policy. This is not as easy to test unless there is an explicit policy rule (such as a 'Taylor Rule'), but the policy might be stated explicitly in the narrative. Finally, it is important to test whether the forediction failure was due to the policy that was implemented. If the model changes when the policy is implemented, then those policy shifts could actually cause forediction failure by themselves. This implies that the model used for policy is invalid, because it is not invariant to the policy change it is being used to analyze.

What exactly do we mean by model invariance? Let's imagine a very simplified story to abstract from the current economic climate. The Bank of England has a model of inflation that depends on whether there is aggregate excess demand in the economy. This is the output gap considered in Chapter 3 . If there is a lot of excess demand in the economy, firms are able to raise their prices as they know that demand exceeds supply, and this puts upward pressure on inflation. The Bank uses the interest rate as its policy variable to control inflation by modifying excess demand. There are a lot of other variables that also influence inflation and excess demand, but just ignore those for the moment. The policy experiment is that a rise in the interest rate will dampen excess demand which in turn lowers inflation. Such a model needs to satisfy the requirement that the relationship between the interest rate and excess demand is not linked to the relationship between excess demand and inflation, in that shifts in the interest rate do not affect the relationship between excess demand and inflation. This is intuitive. Changes in the interest rate should affect inflation via excess demand. If changing the interest rate changes the relationship between inflation and excess demand, we can no longer quantify in advance the effect on inflation of a change in the interest rate. Implementing a policy rise in interest rates would then not have the anticipated outcome, and, if the rise was large, could lead to forecast, and forediction, failure. If so, the policy has been rendered invalid. Fortunately, there are new and innovative approaches to testing for invariance of the policy model to interventions in the past before any new policy changes are implemented, based on the step indicator saturation method we explained in Chapter 9.

The moral here is that simply asserting that your model is 'structural' (in the sense that it correctly captures the properties of the economy), with parameters that are invariant features of how the economy's agent(s) behave, is not a sufficient justification. Theory may propose, but evidence disposes, and failing to follow such a rule is unscientific, but regrettably common in policy-making institutions where models that suffer repeated rejections empirically are stoically maintained despite their entailed policies affecting the lives of millions.

Federal Open Market Committee members' assessments

The Federal Reserve System (Fed) sets US monetary policy by its Federal Open Market Committee (FOMC), which consists of the governors of the

Federal Reserve Board, the president of the New York Fed, and four regional Fed presidents on a rotating basis. The FOMC meets regularly to set its main interest rate, called the Federal Funds Rate. This is the rate at which banks with balances held at the Federal Reserve borrow from one another overnight, which then influences the interest rates that banks set for loans and deposits. The Federal Funds Rate is a key policy lever that feeds through to affect macroeconomic conditions, and is watched worldwide. If the Fed needs to cool the economy, as inflation is starting to take off, say, it would raise interest rates, and vice versa if it wanted to stimulate the economy. The policy instrument takes time to feed through to the macroeconomy, typically with a 1–2 year lag, so forecasts of the state of the macroeconomy are needed well in advance to facilitate policy decisions.

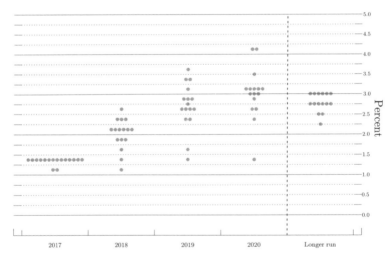

Figure 13.4: FOMC participants' assessments of appropriate monetary policy 2017–2020: midpoints of target range or target level for the Federal Funds rate. Source: Federal Reserve Board.

Since 1992, participants of the Federal Open Market Committee have made twice-yearly forecasts of U.S. inflation, unemployment, and real growth. The intimate link between forecasting and policy decisions is well demonstrated by their 'dot plots'.[8] Such charts show the interest-rate projections of the members of the FOMC for the next four years, as well as a 'longer term' projection looking at where members predict the rate should be when policy is 'normalized' from its current very low levels.

Figure 13.4 reproduces the chart from December 2017. Each 'dot' represents the forecast for one member of the committee of where the rate is expected to be at the end of the calendar year. This is not the member's target rate. Figure 13.4, shows the general trend over the next few years: rates are predicted to increase steadily, before settling at around 3.0%, but the variation in members' predictions is wide, reflecting the diversity of views as well as the difficulty in forecasting any economic variable over such a long time scale.[9]

These charts are one of the most watched news releases of the Fed. The chart demonstrates both direct and indirect links between forecasts and policy. For the direct link, members form predictions not only of the future macroeconomic outlook to inform current policy decisions, but on how the outlook, and hence future policy decisions, will evolve. Indirectly, the path of future rates changes current behavior, for example through current asset prices which are based on future expectations. By communicating the expected path of policy, private-sector expectations of longer-term interest rates can incorporate future expected policy conditions, which should make monetary policy more effective. The argument goes that smaller policy changes are needed as they are augmented by private sector expectations being quickly adjusted. Consequently, greater transparency achieved by publishing these predictions should facilitate more effective monetary policy.

---

[8] See https://www.federalreserve.gov/monetarypolicy/files/fomcprojtabl20171213.pdf

[9] Each shaded circle indicates the value (rounded to the nearest 1/8 percentage point) of an individual participant's judgement of the midpoint of the appropriate target range for the Federal Funds rate or the appropriate target level for the Federal Funds rate at the end of the specifed calendar year or over the longer run. One participant did not submit longer-run projections for the Federal Funds rate.

All that sounds good, but what you will have (hopefully) learnt from our book so far is that forecasts go wrong when location shifts that were not predicted occur during the forecast horizon. Figure 13.5 records an earlier chart from 2015–2018, overlapping Figure 13.4 for 2017 and 2018.

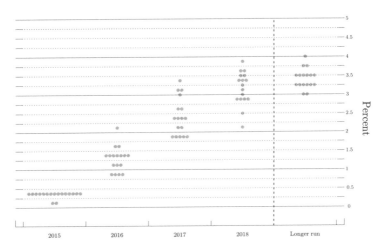

Figure 13.5: FOMC participants' assessments of appropriate monetary policy 2015–2018: midpoints of target range or target level for the Federal Funds rate. Source: Federal Reserve Board.

The first notable feature is the uncanny resemblance between the shapes of the charts: the current year has a near perfect consensus, views then diverge increasingly over the forecast horizon, and anticipate rates rising in the longer run, here through to about 3.5% against 3% in Figure 13.4. However, for the overlapping years, admittedly just 2-years ahead in Figure 13.5, 2017 was predicted to lie between 1.75% and 3%, but ended at 1.25%, a value not predicted by any member, although there is some overlap in the ranges of interest rates for 2018, with the more recent predictions much lower, based on the evidence of slower growth than expected in 2015.

The dot plots of the members projections are conditional on the *current* information set, so as news arrives, these predictions are likely to change. A recent study assesses the value of individual forecasts in a committee-based policy process (using the techniques explained in Chapter 9).[10] It finds that the Federal Reserve Bank presidents and the Federal Reserve Board governors bring distinct complementary information about the U.S. economy to the FOMC meetings, thereby improving forecasting accuracy. Nevertheless, these charts should not be taken as guaranteed forecasts of future policy moves—beware the unknown unknowns if doing so.

---

[10] Ericsson, Hendry, Yanki Kalfa and Jaime Marquez (2018), *The Wisdom of Committees*, Federal Reserve Board of Governors.

Chapter 14

Can you trust economic forecasts?

'If I wasn't real,' Alice said—half-laughing through her tears, it all seemed so ridiculous—'I shouldn't be able to cry.'
'I hope you don't suppose those are real tears?' Tweedledum interrupted in a tone of great contempt.
From Lewis Carroll, *Through the Looking-Glass and What Alice Found There*, London: Macmillan and Co., 1899.

A definition of 'Trust', taken from the Oxford English Dictionary, is 'Firm belief in the reliability, truth, or ability of someone or something; confidence or faith in a person or thing, or in an attribute of a person or thing.' So, if economic forecasts are to be trusted, they need to be reliable and users of economic forecasts must have confidence in them. The word 'confidence' is fundamental here. We use 'confidence bands' to convey the uncertainty associated with a forecast. Forecasts are not required to be precise to be trustworthy, but must be reliable and we must have confidence in them. So why is there a lack of confidence in economic forecasts? This book has explored the many reasons why forecasts may not be accurate, but the uncertainty associated with the economic forecasts needs to be clearly outlined. Systematic forecast failure directly implies that the forecasts are not reliable, so would be inherently untrustworthy. Forecasters need a track record of no systematic mistakes to be thought of as trustworthy with the public.

We have seen from our driver on her journey that many events can thwart the accuracy of her initial forecasts. But the initial forecasts must be able to convey the appropriate uncertainties associated with the journey. If our driver told her friend that her predicted arrival time was in 3 hours time, but, given the uncertainties surrounding possible traffic on route, there was a 50% probability that she could arrive in 4 hours rather than 3, then her friend would not judge her prediction too harshly when she arrived later than the 3 hours initially forecast. The prediction was put into context, so users of the forecasts are well aware that the forecast was just that—a statement about the future, and not a guarantee of an arrival time. Many agencies such as airlines, train and bus companies are required to state both the departure and arrival times of their services, but often with an allowance of some percentage of the journey time before being deemed late (and proudly announcing any early arrivals). If seriously late arrivals become the norm, complaints usually abound, although sometimes spurious 'improvements' are made by increasing the stated journey time.

In economics, forecasts will almost always be wrong to some extent. We are dealing with human behavior that is highly complex and partly unpredictable, facing unanticipated events, with limited information and a lack of accurate data on the phenomena of interest, as well as inherent randomness. As Friedrich Hayek remarked in his Nobel Lecture,[1] economists cannot operate like the physical scientists, where predictions are testable, refutable, and will always hold under well-specified conditions as they are based on laws that account for the observed phenomena as functions of comparatively few variables. However, wrong forecasts in economics should not entail that the forecasts cannot be trusted. The forecasts must come with a clear guide as to the uncertainty associated with them. Perhaps think of these guides as 'health warnings': as seen on pharmaceutical

---

[1] See https://www.nobelprize.org/nobel_prizes/economic-sciences/laureates/1974/hayek-lecture.html.

packages, 'taking paracetamol may leave you feeling drowsy'. An equivalent health warning for any published forecast should clearly state the width of the interval forecasts and the conditioning information used in their preparation. Media that publish headline forecasts with no qualifying uncertainties are partly to blame for public skepticism.

Thirty years on from one of the most embarrassing forecast failures in meteorology in the UK—when Michael Fish stated on national TV that there was no storm on its way, but a few hours later a storm hit, with winds of up to 122mph damaging more than 3 million homes—weather forecasts have become much more accurate. The reputation of weather forecasters is much improved, with more accurate forecasts providing better warning before severe weather systems, as well as dynamically and spatially finer predictions with smaller uncertainties. So how do economists compare to weather forecasters? As the Chief Economist at the Bank of England, Andy Haldane, remarked in discussion at the Institute for Government, meteorological forecasting had improved markedly following that forecasting mistake and the economics profession should follow in its footsteps.[2]

Is economic forecasting an oxymoron?

Episodes of forecast failure naturally question the public's trust in the economic forecasts. But we need to disentangle the reasons why economists have mis-predicted in the past to establish how and why the trust has been broken. When Her Majesty Queen Elizabeth visited the London School of Economics in November 2008, as a second Great Depression was potentially looming large, she asked Professor Luis Garicano, director of research at the LSE's management department a simple but devastating question: why did nobody see it coming? This is a valid question, and one that was asked not only by the Queen but by the public, by politicians, and by many members of the economics profession themselves.

There are lessons to be learned from episodes such as the Financial Crisis, including:

---

[2] https://livestream.com/accounts/5208398/events/6729795/videos/145963063.

- The past is not a reliable guide to the future.

- The consensus is not always right.

- Economic forecasting is *hard*, but is not a 'hard science', even though some claim that it is.

- Recognize wrong models and wrong assumptions before any damage is done.

- Do not defend forecasts when the evidence counters their accuracy.

If our driver repeatedly arrives at her destination one hour late, her friend will cease to have trust in her predictions (although she may learn to just add an hour as an intercept correction). The distrust in economic forecasts arises from past experiences of forecast failure. The public ask; 'Why should we believe you if you've been wrong in the past?' So how can the economics profession regain the trust of the politicians and the public?

In need of better communication

Forecasting is difficult. We need to predict diverse human behavior without the help of a crystal ball. The forecaster needs to be correct about the timing, direction, and magnitude of shifts that will occur from any aspect of a highly complex, non-constant, non-linear system. We might as well give up, we hear you say. But then how do you make any decisions? In Chapter 1, we briefly addressed this issue when Hendry was challenged by a taxi driver in Oslo who eventually agreed that forecasting was essential in his job, once it was clarified that he made forecasts all the time. A 'best guess' of the future outlook is needed for all sorts of decisions, planning, investment, economic policy, etc. Even if we accept that our forecasts will inevitably be wrong, we should do much more to engender trust in economic forecasts. It is incumbent on economists, experts, and the media to improve the explanations accompanying economic forecasts and communicate the forecasts and their associated uncertainties better.

First, economic forecasters must convey the complexity of the global economic system. Returning to Hayek, he makes clear that completely accurate predictions in economics would require complete knowledge of all parts of the universe and all interactions between all parts. Forecasting models can only ever be approximations to their high-dimensional economies, which in turn are part of an even larger global system, and the quality of those approximations will vary over time, across variables, and across horizons. Given such a complicated world, economists must simplify their models thereof, often by aggregation and by assuming that some aspects of the economy are independent of others, and hence can be modeled separately, ignoring interactions. These simplifying assumptions can be dangerous. Witness the exclusion of banks from the macroeconomic models used to forecast prior to the Financial Crisis, so the impacts of bank behavior were not being scrutinized.

Second, forecasters have a responsibility to explain how the forecasts were made. Forecasts are essentially computed by extrapolating current data forward, as we saw in Chapter 2, mediated by expert judgement. However, Chapter 3 noted that we may not know where the economy is currently. A lack of good data on the present state of the economy will mean the forecast commences from the wrong starting point. Statistical revisions to 'where we are' can render forecasts inaccurate for very different reasons than a failure to forecast future movements. Forecasts are dependent on the quality of the data and the degree of regularity in the data, as well as the approach used to build the forecasting model. Also, poor selection methods can lead to poor models and often poor forecasts. For users to have trust in the economic forecasts, they need trust in the agencies producing the data and confidence in the methods used to build the forecasting models as well as in the forecasts themselves. As we discussed above, forecasters often tell 'stories' about their forecasts, what we called foredictions, both to clarify their basis and their likely uncertainties. Such narratives now almost always accompany forecasts that have policy implications, and seek to raise confidence in both the forecasts and the policies they entail.

Third, it is essential to accurately convey the considerable uncertainty in all economic forecasts, even when there are no sudden abrupt shifts.

Different models will have different degrees of uncertainty associated with them. Chapter 4 highlighted that when forecasts are not perfectly accurate, it can be difficult to judge how good, or bad, they are. For example, there is often a disparity in the magnitudes of forecasts between different agencies, despite their direction being consistent across almost all forecasts.

Fourth, uncertainty is a difficult concept to understand and process, the topic of Chapter 5. Point forecasts are reported more commonly than interval or density forecasts because of the ease of conveying a single number relative to a whole distribution. If we were looking at a fan chart for inflation with a two-year horizon central tendency at 2% per annum, and in two years time inflation was running at 5%, we should not immediately assume the forecast failed. Accuracy must be judged relative to the uncertainty. Let's assume that this realization lay outside the widest bands of the fan chart. This is not forecast failure in and of itself. We would expect 1 in every 20 occasions for the forecast to lie outside of 95% bands. Of course, if a string of forecasts fell outside of the bands, then we have forecast failure. But the forecasts need to be judged relative to the associated uncertainty reported with the forecasts. In turn, that requires that usefully accurate forecast intervals are calculated and reported—and we have seen that the uncertainty is itself uncertain.

Fifth, whenever a forecast is reported, it is important to clarify the distinction between conditional and unconditional forecasts. Forecasts often condition on some aspects of the future economic outlook. This may be done by including 'off-line projections' of key variables that are not forecast within the system. Examples of this approach are the Bank of England projections for inflation and output that condition on projections for the Bank Rate, the Sterling Effective Exchange Rate, Oil Prices, Gas Prices and Nominal Government Expenditure.[3] If forecasts fail because such projections transpire to be badly incorrect, that does not impugn the model, but does entail devoting greater care to how off-line projections are made. A closely related issue is that scenario forecasts make different conditioning assumptions to obtain alternative forecasts from the same model.

---

[3] See, for example, the assumptions, the recorded Monetary Policy Committee key judgements, and the indicative projections for the August 2017 *Inflation Report*: http://www.bankofengland.co.uk/publications/Pages/inflationreport/2017/aug.aspx.

Scenarios are a method of exploring counterfactuals, but their projections must be interpreted carefully given the associated conditioning information, especially as any accompanying interval forecasts require models to be invariant across all the scenarios.

Sixth, economic forecasts must also be evaluated *ex post*. Forecast errors can often be explained after the event. Were the errors due to the wrong starting point, revealed by later data revisions; or to using poor models which omitted important relevant factors, requiring improvements to the models by better selection methods; or to incorrect conditioning information, requiring more valid 'givens' to underpin forecasts; or to badly estimated models with the wrong magnitudes or directions of effects within the models, so that updating estimates from more data is needed? Larger errors are probably due to unanticipated events occurring over the forecast horizon, discussed in Chapters 6 and 7, whereas Chapters 8–12 considered how to adapt to, mitigate, or even anticipate, location shifts to help reduce such errors.

Detailed analyses of why forecasts are wrong will improve transparency and accountability and hopefully engender less distrust of economic forecasts in the future. Mis-forecasting one-off events should not erode trust, but evidence of systematic mis-forecasting without learning from past mistakes will leave the environment ripe for criticism and skepticism of future forecasts. We need to make the hedgehog graphs of Chapter 7 obsolete by avoiding systematic mistakes.

Can you believe forecasts from 'experts'?

One of the most divisive events in recent UK history was the referendum for the UK to leave the European Union. During the campaign, one of the key tenets was how the UK economy would look after it left the EU. The difficulty with the question was that there was a large number of economic possibilities ranging from membership of the Single Market and Customs Union to a hard Brexit, all of which had unknown outcomes. A number of well respected bodies, such as the Bank of England, the International Monetary Fund (IMF), the Organisation for Economic Co-operation and

Development (OECD), and the Institute for Fiscal Studies (ISF), produced forecasts, all with similar predictions about the direction of the economy. Michael Gove, then the UK's Justice Secretary, when asked to name a single independent economic authority that thought Brexit was a good idea stated: 'I think that the people of this country have had enough of experts from organisations with acronyms saying ... that they know what is best and getting it consistently wrong, because these people ... are the same ones who got it consistently wrong.'[4] So should we ignore the expertise of economic forecasters and resort to our own crystal balls?

The telling riposte from Lord Gus O'Donnell, previously Head of the UK Civil Service, was simple: 'Good luck to Mr Gove repairing his own car after a breakdown.' This comment was especially forceful as many Britons use the AA or RAC to do so, archetypal organizations with acronyms that fortunately do send experts to the rescue.

Experts bear a responsibility to produce the most accurate forecasts that they can, but the public must recognize that some events are inherently difficult to predict. Forecasts that respond rapidly to a changing environment, that are able to predict transitions after unanticipated events, that carefully explain the uncertainties and conditioning information associated with forecasts, and that utilize the best methods, models and data, are invaluable. To get rid of experts would take us back to the dark ages of forecasting not only in economics, but in many other disciplines including meteorology, leaving us reliant on hunches, guesses, and politicians' whims and fancies, wrecking precisely what Robert Fitzroy set out to achieve.

There is no conclusion to forecasting in a turbulent world. New insights will undoubtedly be discovered to improve our understanding of forecast errors and failures, and better approaches will be invented, both leading to improved practice. But as with the fundamental problem facing forecasting itself, these insights and developments are currently unpredictable.

---

[4]See https://www.youtube.com/watch?v=GGgiGtJk7MA.

Chapter 15

Further reading

A number of other authors have sought to explain forecasting, sometimes called predicting the future, and its problems, most based on the idea behind a quote attributed to Nils Bohr, Physics Nobel Laureate that 'prediction is very difficult, especially if it's about the future'. These include: *Predicting the Future*, essays by famous individuals edited by Leo Howe and Alan Wain, Cambridge University Press (1993); Nate Silver, *The Signal and the Noise: Why so many Predictions Fail–but Some Don't*, Penguin (2012); Philip Tetlock and Dan Gardener, *Superforecasting: The Art and Science of Prediction*, Random House (2015); and *Forewarned: A Sceptics Guide to Prediction* by Paul Goodwin, Blackwell Publishing, 2017. *The Undercover Economist Strikes Back: How to Run or Ruin an Economy*, by Tim Harford, Penguin (2012), makes many amusing points about macroeconomics.

The modern theory of economic forecasting was initiated by Nobel Laureate Trygve Haavelmo (1944), 'The probability approach in econometrics', *Econometrica* **12**. An early text building on Haavelmo' insights is Lawrence Klein, also a Nobel Laureate, *An Essay on the Theory of Economic Prediction*, Markham Publishing Company, 1971. Also Diane Coyle, *GDP: A Brief but Affectionate History*, Princeton University Press, 2001, provides precisely what her title suggests.

For an introduction to economic forecasting, try several of the chapters in D.F. Hendry and N.R. Ericsson, *Understanding Economic Forecasts*, MIT Press, 2001. Two more general textbooks are: C.W.J. Granger and Paul Newbold, *Forecasting Economic Time Series*, Academic Press, 1977, and accidentally copying a great title two decades later, M.P. Clements and D.F. Hendry, *Forecasting Economic Time Series*, Cambridge University Press, 1998, with a more advanced follow up by the same authors in *Forecasting Non-stationary Economic Time Series*, MIT Press, 1999. An earlier approach to forecasting is explained in George Box and Gwilym Jenkins, *Time Series Analysis: Forecasting and Control*, Holden-Day, 1970.

There are a number of handbooks on economic forecasting including four already this century reflecting a resurgence of interest in what was once the orphan of economics: M.P. Clements and D.F. Hendry, *A Companion to Economic Forecasting*, Blackwells, 2002; Graham Elliott, Granger and Allan Timmermann, *Handbook of Econometrics on Forecasting*, Elsevier, 2006; M.P. Clements and D.F. Hendry, *Oxford Handbook of Economic Forecasting*, Oxford University Press, 2011; and, most recently, G. Elliott and A. Timmermann, *Handbook of Economic Forecasting*, North Holland, 2013.

Terence Mills, *Economic Forecasting*, Edward Elgar (2 volumes), 1999, reprints many of the most salient papers on economic forecasting, as does C.W.J. Granger, *Modelling Economic Series*, Clarendon Press, 1990, providing important papers on both forecasting and modeling.

In *Econometrics: Alchemy or Science? Essays in Econometric Methodology*, Blackwell Publishers, 1993, D.F. Hendry outlines the progression of the general-to-specific (*Gets*) methodology from its inception in the research of Ted Anderson and Denis Sargan. Julia Campos, Neil Ericsson, and D.F. Hendry, *General-to-specific Modelling*, Edward Elgar, 2005, provide an extensive discussion and reprint many of the key papers in the literature. The current generation of automatic *Gets* modeling is *Autometrics* in *PcGive*: see Jurgen Doornik, '*Autometrics*', in J.L. Castle and Neil Shephard (eds.), *The Methodology and Practice of Econometrics*, Oxford University Press, 2009; and J.A. Doornik and D.F. Hendry, *Empirical Econometric Modelling using PcGive*, 8th edition, Timberlake Consultants Press, 2018. D.F. Hendry and J.A. Doornik, *Empirical Model*

Discovery and Theory Evaluation, MIT Press, 2014, provide an up-to-date treatment of the theory with applications.

The model of UK M1 demand in Chapters 2 and 11 is discussed in D.F. Hendry and N.R. Ericsson, (1991), 'Modeling the demand for narrow money in the United Kingdom and the United States', *European Economic Review*, **35**. James Tobin, (1950), 'A statistical demand function for food in the U.S.A.', *Journal of the Royal Statistical Society A*, **113**(2) presented the original food demand analysis, and Jan Magnus and Mary Morgan, *Methodology and Tacit Knowledge: Two Experiments in Econometrics*, John Wiley and Sons, 1999, orchestrated the newer analyses of the problem noted in Chapter 9. The Chapter 11 model of UK real wages is presented in J.L. Castle and D.F. Hendry 'Semi-automatic non-linear model selection', Chapter 7 in Haldrup, N., Meitz, M. and Saikkonen, P. (eds.) *Essays in Nonlinear Time Series Econometrics*, Oxford University Press, 2014. The model of hurricane damages is from A.B. Martinez, (2017), 'How quickly can we adapt to change? An assessment of hurricane damage mitigation efforts using forecast uncertainty', Oxford Economics Working Paper, 831.

Anindya Banerjee, Juan Dolado, John Galbraith, and D.F. Hendry, *Co-integration, Error Correction and the Econometric Analysis of Non-Stationary Data*, Oxford University Press, 1993, provide a textbook explanation of stochastic non-stationarity.

Some papers relevant to non-economics topics include that by Roberto Scarpa, (2001), 'Predicting volcanic eruptions', *Science* **293** who lists Pinatubo, Philippines, in 1991, Rabaul, New Guinea, in 1994, and Soufriere Hills, Montserrat, in 1995 as examples of successful forecasts of volcanic activity. Also Ross Stein, Aykut Barka, and James Dieterich in their 1997 paper 'Progressive failure on the North Anatolian fault since 1939 by earthquake stress triggering', *Geophysical Journal International* **128** provide predictions of the 1999 earthquake at İzmit on the Anatolian fault. Aurélia Hubert-Ferrari, Aykut Barka, Eric Jacques, Süleyman Nalbant, Bertrand Meyer, Ronaldo Armijo, Paul Tapponnier, and Geoffrey King (2000), 'Seismic hazard in the Marmara Sea region following the 17 August 1999 İzmit earthquake', *Nature* **404**, discuss the outcome of that prediction *ex post*.

For investigations of the 2004 Indian Ocean tsunami see the work, by James Holliday, John Rundle, Kristy Tiampo, and Donald Turcotte, (2006), 'Using earthquake intensities to forecast earthquake occurrence times', *Nonlinear Processes in Geophysics* **13**, who show that stress tension in that subduction region was measurable, and, although the undersea earthquake was recorded by an automatic satellite system, such information was not seen at the time. The Deep-ocean assessment and reporting of tsunamis (DART) system was developed by the US NOAA Pacific Marine Environmental Laboratory, and is able to detect tsunamis as small as one centimeter, reporting back in real-time to provide site-specific predictions of tsunami impacts on coasts.

Index